Debora M. Coty

EVERYDAY
Hope

Spiritual Refreshment
for Women

BARBOUR
PUBLISHING

Scripture quotations marked NLT are taken from the *Holy Bible*, New Living Translation, copyright © 1996, 2004. Used by permission of Tyndale House Publishers, Inc., Wheaton, Illinois 60189, U.S.A. All rights reserved.

Scripture quotations marked MSG are from *THE MESSAGE*. Copyright © by Eugene H. Peterson 1993, 1994, 1995, 1996, 2000, 2001, 2002. Used by permission of NavPress Publishing Group.

Scripture quotations marked CEV are from the Contemporary English Version, Copyright © 1991, 1992, 1995 by American Bible Society. Used by permission.

Scripture quotations marked NASB are taken from the New American Standard Bible, © 1960, 1962, 1963, 1968, 1971, 1972, 1973, 1975, 1977, 1995 by The Lockman Foundation. Used by permission.

Scripture quotations marked NIV are taken from the HOLY BIBLE, NEW INTERNATIONAL VERSION®. NIV®. Copyright © 1973, 1978, 1984 by International Bible Society. Used by permission of Zondervan. All rights reserved.

Scripture quotations marked KJV are taken from the King James Version of the Bible.

Scripture quotations marked NKJV are taken from the New King James Version®. Copyright © 1982 by Thomas Nelson, Inc. Used by permission. All rights reserved.

Cover design: Kirk DouPonce, DogEared Design

Published by Barbour Publishing, Inc., P.O. Box 719, Uhrichsville, Ohio 44683, www.barbourbooks.com.

Our mission is to publish and distribute inspirational products offering exceptional value and biblical encouragement to the masses.

Member of the
Evangelical Christian
Publishers Association

Printed in India.

Contents

Introduction

Now may our Lord
Jesus Christ who has loved us
and given us eternal comfort
and good hope by grace,
comfort and strengthen your hearts.
2 THESSALONIANS 2:16–17 NASB

Hope isn't just an emotion; it's a perspective, a discipline, a way of life. Hope is a journey of choice. For believers, hope is vital to a dynamic, thriving faith. . .one of the big three that will remain to the end of time: faith, hope, and love (1 Corinthians 13:13).

Hope is a glimmer in the darkness, the buttercup lifting its delicate head from a charred field, that supernatural nudge to persevere when all seems lost. Hope, dear sisters, is simply Jesus. I pray that you find Him in these pages.

5

Abundant Life

Dancing in the Puddles

And so, Lord,
where do I put my hope?
My only hope is in you.

PSALM 39:7 NLT

They say you can tell a lot about a person's foundation of hope by the way she handles a rainy day. Does she turn into a Gloomy Gussy, wailing, "Oh, woe is me. . ." or does she make the best of a bad situation? A hope-filled person will realize that abundant life in Christ isn't about simply enduring the storm but also about learning to dance in the puddles. So grab your galoshes, and let's boogie!

Walking Faith

"Be strong and courageous, and act;
do not fear nor be dismayed,
for the Lord God,
my God, is with you.
He will not fail you nor forsake you."

1 Chronicles 28:20 NASB

What a life verse! What a creed to live by! We are assured that our God will never leave us or forsake us. We draw strength and courage from this assurance and are then able to act; to share our faith boldly—without fear—because we are never alone. The Lord God—our God—is with us.

Shouts of Joy

He will yet fill your mouth
with laughter and your lips
with shouts of joy.

JOB 8:21 NIV

Do you remember the last time you laughed till you cried? For many of us, it's been far too long. Stress tends to steal our joy, leaving us humorless and oh-so-serious. But lightness and fun haven't disappeared forever. They may be buried beneath the snow of a long, wintery life season, but spring is coming, girls. Laughter will bloom again, and our hearts will soar as our lips shout with joy. Grasp that hope!

Attitude

Interior Decorator

> You, O Lord,
> are a shield about me, my glory,
> and the One who lifts my head.
>
> PSALM 3:3 NASB

Have you ever caught a glimpse of yourself reflected in a window and were shocked at the hangdog image you unwittingly portrayed? Slumped shoulders, drooping head, defeated expression? You can straighten your posture and adjust your face, but if the change doesn't come from the inside out, it won't stick.

God is our Interior Decorator. Only He can provide that inner joy that projects outward and lifts our heads.

Invite Him in to work on your place.

9

Designer Label

We wish that each of you
would always be eager to show how
strong and lasting your hope really is.

HEBREWS 6:11 CEV

Our behavior is always on display and, like it or not, we are judged by our actions. . .and inactions. Without an explanation for our behavior—that we're motivated by faith to be Christlike—people will make up their own ideas: Her mama taught her right; she was just born nice; she acts sweet so everyone will like her. Isn't it better to be up-front and give credit to the One we're emulating?

Wear the label of your Designer proudly.

I'm No Eeyore

Then [Job's] wife said to him,
"Do you still hold fast your
integrity? Curse God and die!"

JOB 2:9 NASB

Job's wife was the unwilling recipient of
Satan's attacks because of her husband's
righteous life. When the going got tough,
our girl lost faith and hope disintegrated.
We, too, sometimes lose sight of all God
has done for us and focus only on what He
hasn't done. Our optimistic attitudes are
consumed by negativity. Job's response
is the key to escaping the shackles of
Eeyore-ism: "I know that my Redeemer
lives" (Job 19:25 NASB).

Beauty

Inside-Out Love

God has made everything beautiful
for its own time.

ECCLESIASTES 3:11 NLT

Beauty is a concern of every woman to
some degree. We worry about hair, makeup,
weight, fashions. But real beauty can only
come from God's inside-out love. Once we
are able to finally comprehend His infinite
and extravagant love for us—despite our
flat feet and split ends—our heart glow will
reflect radiant beauty from the inside out.
Only when we feel truly loved are we free to
be truly lovely.

Confounded Corsets

Cultivate inner beauty,
the gentle, gracious kind
that God delights in.

1 PETER 3:4 MSG

In our quest for beauty, we buy into all sorts of crazy things: mud facials, cosmetic surgery, body piercings, obsessive dieting, squeezing size 10 feet into size 8 shoes. The image of Scarlett O'Hara's binding corset makes us shudder. (Reminds me of a pair of jeans I wrestled with just last week.) Yet God's idea of beauty is on the inside—where spandex cannot touch. Let's resolve to devote more time pursuing inner beauty that will never require Botox.

Good Enough

Leah's eyes were weak, but Rachel was beautiful of form and face.

GENESIS 29:17 NASB

Have you ever felt like a booby prize? No doubt Leah did. Hunky Jacob labored seven years to marry Leah's gorgeous sister, Rachel. Then their squirrelly father switched his daughters at the altar. Jacob freaked. Leah tanked. We, too, sometimes feel that we're not good enough—that we don't measure up. But Leah gave birth to six of the twelve tribes of Israel, the cornerstone of Judeo-Christendom.

God has a mighty plan for all of us Leahs.

Granter of Dreams

Hope deferred makes the heart sick,
but a dream fulfilled is a tree of life.

PROVERBS 13:12 NLT

As a teenager, I dreamed of one day writing a book. But life intervened, and I became a wife, mother, occupational therapist, and piano teacher. My writing dream was shelved. Twenty-five years later, after my youngest chick flew the coop, God's still, small voice whispered, "It's time." Within five years, the Granter of Dreams delivered over seventy articles and nine book contracts. What's your dream? Be brave and take the first step.

Everyday Blessings

But the eyes of the LORD are
on those who fear him, on those
whose hope is in his unfailing love.

PSALM 33:18 NIV

The Lord of all creation is watching our
every moment and wants to fill us with His
joy. He often interrupts our lives with His
blessings: butterflies dancing in sunbeams,
dew-touched spiderwebs, cotton candy
clouds, and glorious crimson sunsets. The
beauty of His creation reassures us of His
unfailing love and fills us with hope. But it is
up to us to take the time to notice.

Burning Out

Stop the Roller Coaster

Why am I discouraged?
Why is my heart so sad?
I will put my hope in God!
PSALM 43:5 NLT

For women, ruts of depression are often caused by careening hormones. Rampaging hormones can cause us to spend countless hours weeping without knowing why—or bite someone's head off, lose precious sleep, or sprout funky nervous habits. Knowing that this hormonally-crazed state is only temporary, we must intentionally place our hope in tomorrow and pray that God will turn the downside up!

My Refuge

God is our refuge and strength,
always ready to help
in times of trouble.

PSALM 46:1 NLT

What is your quiet place? The place you go to get away from the fray, to chill out, think, regroup, and gain perspective? Mine is a hammock nestled beneath a canopy of oaks in my backyard. . .nobody around but birds, squirrels, an occasional wasp, God, and me. There I can pour out my heart to my Lord, hear His comforting voice, and feel His strength refresh me. We all need a quiet place. God, our refuge, will meet us there.

A Little Goes a Long Way

"The LORD our God has allowed a few
of us to survive as a remnant."

 EZRA 9:8 NLT

Remnants. Useless by most standards, but God is in the business of using tiny slivers of what's left to do mighty things. Nehemiah rebuilt the fallen walls of Jerusalem with a remnant of Israel; Noah's three sons repopulated the earth after the flood; four slave boys—Daniel, Shadrach, Meshach, and Abednego—kept faith alive for an entire nation. When it feels as if bits and pieces are all that has survived of your hope, remember how much God can accomplish with remnants!

Character

Stinkin' Thinkin'

Let us be sober, having put on the breastplate of faith and love, and as a helmet, the hope of salvation.

1 THESSALONIANS 5:8 NASB

Women's hats aren't as popular as they once were, but you wouldn't know it by my closet. I love accessorizing with a perky hat to make a statement, to disguise a bad hair day, or to keep my brain from sautéing in the sizzling Florida sun. The Bible says we need to protect our minds from bad spiritual rays, too. Nasty input produces nasty output: stinkin' thinkin'. When we're tempted to input a questionable movie or book, let's don our salvation helmets and say, "No way!"

Redeeming Pain

I may have fallen,
but I will get up;
I may be sitting in the dark,
but the LORD is my light.

MICAH 7:8 CEV

"Life is pain, Highness. Anyone who says differently is selling something." This memorable line from the movie, *The Princess Bride*, rings true. Pain is inevitable in life, but God can use it for redemptive purposes. Pain can knock us down, cast us into darkness, and make us feel defeated. But it's only as debilitating as we allow it to be. We will get up again; we will learn, adapt, and grow through redeeming pain.

Maid of Honor

*For I fully expect and hope that. . .
my life will bring honor to Christ,
whether I live or die.*

PHILIPPIANS 1:20 NLT

Honor. A word not as respected in our
society as it once was. In these days of
suggestive attire, cohabitation without
marriage, and tolerance for every behavior
imaginable, it's hard to remember what
honor means. As Christians, our hope and
expectation is to honor Christ with our
lives—especially in the details—because we
are the only reflection of Jesus some people
might ever see.

The SAM Creed

If we are thrown into the blazing furnace, the God we serve is able to save us. . . . But even if he does not. . .we will never serve your gods.

DANIEL 3:17–18 NLT

Shadrach, Meshach, and Abednego were Israeli boys who were captured and transported as slaves to Babylon. Ordered by their new king to worship his god or die horribly in a fiery furnace, the boys evoked the SAM Creed, an acronym for their names: My God is able to deliver me, but even if He chooses not to, I will still follow Him. Through tough times, let's resolve to live by The SAM Creed.

See Ya, Self

"Blessed are the poor in spirit,
for theirs is the kingdom of heaven."

MATTHEW 5:3 NASB

We don't often think of ourselves as "poor in spirit," but this passage refers to those who are not full of themselves; those who are filled instead with God's spirit. "Poor" in this context means selfless rather than selfish; those with an attitude of dependence on God. How do we become poor in spirit and revel in the hope and promise of heaven? By emptying ourselves of self and the pride of self-sufficiency, and refilling ourselves with Jesus.

Loose Lips

We all make many mistakes.
For if we could control our
tongues, we would be perfect
and could also control ourselves
in every other way.

JAMES 3:2 NLT

Many of us don't let thoughts marinate
long before we spew them out of our mouths.
We want to honor God with our speech but
seem to spend more time dousing forest
fires resulting from sparks kindled by our
wagging tongues (James 3:5). Don't despair!
There's hope for loose lips! The
Creator of self-control is happy
to loan us a muzzle (Psalm 39:1)
if we sincerely want to change.

Cat-a-tude Versus Dog-a-tude

May those who hope in you not be
disgraced because of me,
O Lord, the LORD Almighty.

PSALM 69:6 NIV

Are you a hisser or a wagger?

Perhaps you have a feline attitude: It's all about me. I like you for what you can do for me. You'll have my attention only when it's convenient for me. Me, me, me.

Or maybe you have a dog mentality: It's all about you. I love you unconditionally just because you're you. How can I make you happy? God is glorified by selflessness, not selfishness. Let's strive to make our Master proud.

It'll Be All Right

Our comfort is abundant
through Christ.

2 CORINTHIANS 1:5 NASB

As children, there's no greater comfort
than running to Mommy or Daddy and
hearing, "It'll be all right." As adults, when
we're frightened, dismayed, or dispirited, we
yearn to run to enveloping arms for the same
comfort. Abba Father—Papa God—is waiting
with open arms to offer us loving comfort
in our times of need. If we listen closely,
we'll hear His still, small voice speak to our
hearts: "It'll be all right, my child."

I Am His

My health may fail,
and my spirit may grow weak,
but God remains the strength
of my heart; he is mine forever.

PSALM 73:26 NLT

My dear friend was dying of an inoperable brain tumor. Mother of three, 48-year-old Sherill could no longer walk or care for herself, yet her voice was filled with hope as she gazed unwaveringly into my eyes and quoted this verse. She added something very significant at the end that I'll hold close to my heart and draw strength from when my time comes: "He is mine forever…and I am His."

Comforting the Comfortless

He brings us alongside someone
else who is going through hard
times so that we can be there for that
person just as God was there for us.

2 CORINTHIANS 1:4 MSG

Heartbroken and hollow after my sixth miscarriage, I struggled to find meaning in my loss. My heavenly Father's arms comforted me when I burst into tears at song lyrics or at the sight of a mother cuddling her infant in Wal-Mart. I finally relinquished my babies to Jesus' loving embrace, confident that I'd see them again one day. I was then able to share His comfort and hope with other women suffering miscarriages.

Contentment

Increasing Visibility

"Where then is my hope?"
JOB 17:15 NIV

On hectic days when fatigue takes its toll, when we feel like cornless husks, hope disappears. When hurting people hurt people, and we're in the line of fire, hope vanishes. When ideas fizzle, efforts fail; when we throw the spaghetti against the wall and nothing sticks, hope seems lost. But we must remember it's only temporary. The mountaintop isn't gone just because it's obscured by fog. Visibility will improve tomorrow and hope will rise.

The Eyes Have It

All of you together are Christ's body,
and each one of you is a part of it.

1 CORINTHIANS 12:27 NLT

Just as our bodies are compiled of many
parts, each essential for functioning as
a whole, the body of Christ is made up of
hands, feet, ears, hearts, and minds. We
women understand this concept but tend
to compare ourselves to others. If we're
hands, we wish we were feet. If we're noses,
we'd rather be eyes. Sometimes we feel
like bunions. But God views us as equally
important, none better than another.
Even us toenails!

Wag More

I am not complaining
about having too little.
I have learned to be satisfied
with whatever I have.

PHILIPPIANS 4:11 CEV

I oozed envy as writer buddies received awards, broke sales records, and snagged lucrative contracts. What about me? Where were my accolades? It had always been enough to know I was following God's chosen path for me, but suddenly all I could do was complain. I wanted more.

Then God sent me a sign. Actually, it was a bumper sticker on a passing car: WAG MORE, BARK LESS. Message received. . .with a smile.

Courage

Lord of the Dance

Remember your promise to me;
it is my only hope.

PSALM 119:49 NLT

The Bible contains many promises from
God: He will protect us (Proverbs 1:33),
comfort us (2 Corinthians 1:5), help in
our times of trouble (Psalm 46:1), and
encourage us (Isaiah 40:29). The word
encourage comes from the root phrase
"to inspire courage." Like an earthly father
encouraging his daughter from backstage
as her steps falter during her dance
recital, our Papa God wants to
inspire courage in us, if we
only look to Him.

Holding Hands

When I am afraid,
I will put my trust in You.

PSALM 56:3 NASB

While I cowered in a bathroom stall before
my first speaking event, my queasy stomach
rolled and sweat beaded on my forehead.
I prayed for a way to escape. Into my head
popped a childhood memory verse: "When
I am afraid, I will put my trust in You." My
pounding heart calmed. I repeated the
scripture aloud and felt my nausea subside
and panic diminish. Peace flooded my soul.
When we're afraid, Papa God is right beside
us holding our hand.

Bigger than Fear

Having hope will give you courage.
You will be protected
and will rest in safety.

JOB 11:18 NLT

Tossing, turning, sleepless nights: What
woman doesn't know these intimately?
Our thoughts race with the "what if's"
and fear steals our peace. How precious is
God's promise that He will rescue us from
nagging, faceless fear and give us courage to
just say no to anxious thoughts that threaten
to terrorize us at our most vulnerable
moments. He is our hope and protector.
He is bigger than fear. Anxiety flees in His
presence. Rest with Him tonight.

Daily Walk

Light My Fire

If God is for us,
who can be against us?
ROMANS 8:31 NIV

Some days it feels as if the entire world is conspiring to make us as miserable as possible. Your spouse is crabby, the kids forget to mention the four dozen cupcakes they volunteered you for today, traffic jams, your boss is on the rampage, your coworkers are in nasty moods, you forgot to defrost dinner, the car overheats again. But our God is King of the Universe, and He's on our side. Girl, if that doesn't light your fire, the wood's wet.

Acing the Test

Always be ready to give
an answer when someone
asks you about your hope.

1 PETER 3:15 CEV

Remember algebra tests in high school?
Instant sweat and heart palpitations. You
dreaded going into them unprepared.
You wanted to have answers ready so you
wouldn't be left with saliva drooling from
your gaping mouth when questioned. The
Bible says we should be prepared when
someone asks about the hope within us—the
hope they couldn't help but notice
radiating from our souls. The
answer scores an A+ for all
eternity: Jesus!

Chef d'oeuvre

Be strong and let your heart take courage, all you who hope in the LORD.

PSALM 31:24 NASB

Identical eggs can be turned into greasy fried egg sandwiches or an exquisite soufflé. The difference is how much beating they endure.

When life seems to be beating us down, we must remember that we are a masterpiece in progress. The mixing, slicing, and dicing may feel brutal at times, but our Lord has offered us His courage and strength to endure until He is ready to unveil the chef d'oeuvre.

Down with Flab

Workouts in the gymnasium
are useful, but a disciplined life
in God is far more so, making you
fit both today and forever.

1 TIMOTHY 4:7–8 MSG

Do you have Dumbo flaps? You know, those fleshy wings that hang on the underside of your arms when you raise them. A stiff wind could create liftoff. They say regular workouts will tighten those puppies up. . . and significantly reduce wind shear. Just as we exercise muscles to make them strong, we keep our faith in shape by exercising it. Discipline is the way to conquer flab— physically and spiritually!

Smiling in the Darkness

The hopes of the godless evaporate.

JOB 8:13 NLT

Hope isn't just an emotion; it's a perspective, a discipline, a way of life. It's a journey of choice. We must learn to override those messages of discouragement, despair, and fear that assault us in times of trouble and press toward the light. Hope is smiling in the darkness. It's confidence that faith in God's sovereignty amounts to something. . . something life-changing, life-saving, and eternal.

Let Me Be

"Martha..., you are worried
and upset about many things,
but only one thing is needed.
Mary has chosen what is better."

LUKE 10:41–42 NIV

Martha zipped around cleaning, cooking,
and organizing. Meanwhile, Mary sat at
Jesus' feet. Many of us think like Martha.
Will food magically appear on the table?
Will the house clean itself? We're slaves
to endless to-do lists. Our need to do
overwhelms our desire to be. Constipated
calendars attest that we are human
doings instead of human beings.
But Jesus taught that Mary chose
best—simply to be. Lord, help
this doer learn to be.

Dependence on God

Superglue Faith

In Him, you also, after listening
to the message of truth,
the gospel of your salvation—having
also believed, you were sealed in Him
with the Holy Spirit of promise.

EPHESIANS 1:13 NASB

Remember the old commercial that depicted a construction worker dangling in midair, the top of his helmet bonded by superglue to a horizontal beam? Faith is like superglue. We cling to our God, our foundation, our beam. As believers, we are sealed in Christ, and the bond cannot be undone. Through prayer in times of despair, our faith is strengthened and becomes waterproof, pressure-resistant, and unbreakable.

Small but Mighty

He has...exalted the humble.

LUKE 1:52 NLT

God delights in making small things great. He's in the business of taking scrap-heap people and turning them into treasures: Noah (the laughing stock of his city), Moses (stuttering shepherd turned national leader), David (smallest among the big and powerful), Sarah (old and childless), Mary (poor teenager), Rahab (harlot turned faith-filled ancestor of Jesus). So you and I can rejoice with hope! Let us glory in our smallness!

Pick Me Up, Daddy

*We rejoice in the hope
of the glory of God.*

ROMANS 5:2 NIV

To rejoice means to live joyfully. . .
joy-*fully*. . .full of joy. Joy is a decision we
make. A choice not to keep wallowing in the
mud of our lives. And there will be mud—at
one time or another. When spiritual rain
mixes with the dirt of fallen people, mud
is the inevitable result. The Creator of
sparkling sunbeams, soaring eagles, and
spectacular fuchsia sunsets wants to lift us
out of the mud. Why don't we raise our arms
to Him today?

Encouragement

Keep Breathing, Sister!

As long as we are alive,
we still have hope, just as a live
dog is better off than a dead lion.
ECCLESIASTES 9:4 CEV

Isn't this a tremendous scripture? At first glance, the ending elicits a chuckle. But consider the truth it contains: Regardless of how powerful, regal, or intimidating a lion is, when he's dead, he's dead. But the living—you and I—still have hope. Limitless possibilities! Hope for today and for the future. Although we may be as lowly dogs, fresh, juicy bones abound. As long as we're breathing, it's not too late!

It's a Mystery

This is the day which
the LORD has made;
let us rejoice and be glad in it.

PSALM 118:24 NASB

Let's face it, girls, some mornings our
rejoicing lasts only until the toothpaste
drips onto our new shirt or the toast sets
off the fire alarm. But the mystery of
Jesus-joy is that it's not dependent on rosy
circumstances. If we, after cleaning the shirt
and scraping the toast, intentionally give our
day to the Lord, He will infuse it with His
joy. Things look much better through
Jesus-joy contact lenses!

Dwelling Place

Do you not know that you are
a temple of God and that the
Spirit of God dwells in you?

1 CORINTHIANS 3:16 NASB

Have you ever been awed by the beauty of
a majestic cathedral with towering ceilings
inlaid with gold and silver, magnificent
paintings, rich carpets, and stained glass
windows? Only the finest for the house of
God Almighty.

Did you know God thinks of you
and me as living cathedrals—dwelling
places of His Spirit? How amazing to be
considered worthy of such an honor! How
immeasurable His love to choose us as
His dwelling place!

Endurance

Going the Distance

[David]. . .chose five smooth stones
from the stream. . .and, with his sling
in his hand, approached the Philistine.

1 Samuel 17:40 NIV

That little dude David had no intention
of backing down from his fight until it was
finished. Notice he picked up five rocks,
not just one. He was prepared to go the
distance against his giant. He fully expected
God to make him victorious, but he knew it
wouldn't be easy.

So you've used your first rock against
your giant. Maybe even your second. But
don't give up. Keep reloading your sling and
go the distance. Victory is sweet!

Top Off My Tank

"My grace is sufficient for you,
for my power is made perfect
in weakness."

2 CORINTHIANS 12:9 NIV

There is no weaker vessel than a
bedraggled mother at 6 a.m., staring into a
bathroom mirror after another rough night.
She's trying to decide if the dark smudges
beneath her eyes are yesterday's grape jelly
when she suddenly realizes she's brushing
her hair with her toothbrush. Yep, we are
a sisterhood of slightly sagging spiritual
warriors, but we can depend on
God to power our weak vessels.
And He is able.

Enduring with Grace

Endurance builds character,
which gives us a hope that
will never disappoint us.

ROMANS 5:4–5 CEV

Heroes come in all packages. My 18-year-old niece, Andie, has cerebral palsy and is legally blind. It takes her four times longer than the average person to do just about anything. But she does it anyway: playing drums, walking in leg braces, attending college. Some days, the frustration of being different overwhelms her. But through endurance, she has developed inspiring character traits—rock solid faith, contagious hope, and a stellar sense of humor.

When I grow up, I want to be like Andie.

Heavyweight

This hope is like a firm and steady anchor for our souls.

HEBREWS 6:19 CEV

Julia and Mark anchored their sailboat to do a little reef exploring while they went diving. When they surfaced, the boat was a speck on the horizon. It had drifted more than a half-mile because their anchor was too light.

Hope in Christ is an anchor for our souls. But if the anchor isn't weighted by firm and steady faith, we may drift in strong currents of doubt, problems, and disillusionment. Weigh your anchor today.

Brick by Brick

So then faith cometh by hearing,
and hearing by the word of God.

ROMANS 10:17 KJV

Words are powerful. They cut. They heal.
They confirm. God uses His Word to help us,
to mold us, to make us more like Him. Our
faith is built from the bricks of God's Word.
Brick by brick, we erect, strengthen, and
fortify that faith. But only if we truly listen
and hear the Word of God.

A Perfect Fit

The LORD is good to those
whose hope is in him,
to the one who seeks him.

LAMENTATIONS 3:25 NIV

Seeking God is, for some, like a child
groping in a dark room for the light switch.
She knows it's there, she just can't seem to
put her fingers on it. Some search for God
all their lives, trying on various religions
like pairs of shoes. This one pinches. That
one chafes. But we must bypass religious
fluff for the heart of the matter: Jesus. The
only way to God is through faith in
Christ (John 14:6). Suddenly,
the shoe fits!

Family

Roots

"There is hope for your future,"
declares the LORD,
"And your children will return
to their own territory."
JEREMIAH 31:17 NASB

Prodigal. The word alone evokes an involuntary shudder.

Most of us know parents whose children have left home in the throes of rebellion. Some of us are those parents. After years of protecting and nurturing our children, heartache replaces harmony, panic supersedes pride. But the Great Peacemaker declares that prodigals will one day return to their roots. One of His greatest parables reinforces that hope (Luke 15).

Legacy of Love

After all, when the Lord Jesus
appears, who else but you will give
us hope and joy and be like
a glorious crown for us?

1 THESSALONIANS 2:19 CEV

The most hope-inspiring legacy we can
pass on to the next generation is faith.
What delight it is for us as women to plant
and nurture seeds of faith in our children,
knowing that at harvest they'll stand by our
sides before the Lord Jesus! It's never too
late to till the fertile soil of their hearts by
our example of daily Bible reading, prayer,
and dependence on our Savior.

I've Got a Name

I have redeemed you;
I have called you by your name;
you are Mine.

ISAIAH 43:1 NKJV

Parents have the indescribable privilege of bestowing a name on their newborn. The identity that little person will be known by for the rest of his or her life. In effect, we give them a part of us. They are an extension of ourselves—our flesh, our blood.

Your heavenly Father has called you by name. He has given you part of Himself: Jesus. You are special to Him. You are His daughter. In this, find security. . . comfort. . .hope.

Father God

Jets and Submarines

No power in the sky above or in the earth below. . .will ever be able to separate us from the love of God that is revealed in Christ Jesus our Lord.

ROMANS 8:39 NLT

Have you ever been diving amid the spectacular array of vivid color and teeming life in the silent world under the sea? Painted fish of rainbow hues are backlit by diffused sunbeams. Multi-textured coral dot the gleaming white sand. You honestly feel as if you're in another world. But every world is God's world. He soars above the clouds with us and spans the depths of the seas. Nothing can separate us from His love.

His Little Girls

Just as a father has compassion
on his children, so the LORD has
compassion on those who fear Him.

PSALM 103:13 NASB

Plagued with horrible recurring
nightmares during my childhood, I
remember the terror of waking up
screaming, hair sweat-plastered to my
face. Then like a candle in the darkness,
my father would appear at my bedside, lie
beside me, and gently rub my back until I
fell asleep. Our heavenly Father is like that—
tender, caring, protective. And He, too,
responds when His little girls need
comfort from His loving presence.

His Heart's Delight

The LORD's delight is in those
who fear him, those who put
their hope in his unfailing love.

PSALM 147:11 NLT

Do you remember how you felt when you
witnessed your baby's first faltering steps?
Delight. That's what it was. Just like when
you heard her sing "Jesus Loves Me" in her
squeaky, off-key voice, or she served you
tea in tiny pink teacups. The Bible says the
Lord delights in us, His children, the very
same way. We warm His heart and bring a
smile to His lips when we honor Him with
our lives. He delights in us.

Fatigue

Rest Stop

So let's not allow ourselves
to get fatigued doing good.
At the right time we will harvest a
good crop if we don't give up, or quit.

GALATIANS 6:9 MSG

As women, we're used to serving others.
It's part of the feminine package. But
sometimes we get burned out. Fatigued.
Overburdened. Girls, God doesn't want us
to be washed-out dishrags, to be so boggled
that we try to pay for groceries with our
Blockbuster card. It's up to us to recognize
the symptoms and rest, regroup, reenergize.
This is not indulgent; it's necessary to
do our best in His name. So give yourself
permission to rest. Today.

Let the Sun Shine In

Come to me, all you
who are weary and burdened,
and I will give you rest.

MATTHEW 11:28 NIV

Nothing chokes hope like weariness. Day in and day out drudgery produces weariness of body, heart, and soul. It feels like dark clouds have obscured the sun and cast us into perpetual shadow. But Jesus promised rest for our weary souls, respite from our burdens, and healing for our wounds. . .if we come to Him. The sun isn't really gone, it's just hidden until the clouds roll away.

Fear

No Wimps Here

For God has not given us a spirit
of fear and timidity, but of power,
love, and self-discipline.

2 TIMOTHY 1:7 NLT

Do you suffer paralysis by analysis? Are you so afraid of trying something new that you put it off until you can think it through. . . and end up doing nothing at all? Too much introspection creates inertia, and we abhor the ineffective wimps we become. Sisters, God never intended for us to be wimps. His power and love are available to replace our fear and infuse us with courage. Shake off that paralysis and get moving!

Battle Plan

I sought the LORD,
and He answered me,
and delivered me from all my fears.

PSALM 34:4 NASB

There is nothing more wasteful than fear. Fear paralyzes, destroys potential, and shatters hope. It's like an enemy attacking from our blind side. But we don't have to allow fear to defeat us. It's a war that we can win! First comes earnest prayer, then comes change. God will deliver us from our fears if we seek Him and follow His battle plan.

They're Just Men

"He may have a great army,
but they are merely men.
We have the LORD our God to help
us and to fight our battles for us!"

2 CHRONICLES 32:8 NLT

When facing attack from an enemy army, Hezekiah uttered these profound words: "They're just men. The God of all creation is standing by to fight for us! No comparison!" And sure enough, against all human reasoning, God sent an angel to defeat the entire enemy army (2 Chronicles 32:21). God still intervenes today to help us fight our battles, whether supernaturally or by natural means. Trust Him. He's got His armor on.

Go for It

When everything was hopeless,
Abraham believed anyway,
deciding to live. . .on what
God said he would do.

ROMANS 4:18 MSG

Y ou can't do that. It's impossible." Have you
ever been told this? Or just thought it because
of fear or a previous experience with failure?

This world is full of those who
discourage rather than encourage. If we
believe them, we'll never do anything. But
if we, like Abraham, believe that God has
called us for a particular purpose, we'll go
for it despite our track records.
Past failure doesn't dictate
future failure. If God wills it,
He fulfills it.

Feelings

When I'm Baaad

"I am the good shepherd;
I know my own sheep, and
they know me, just as my Father
knows me and I know the Father."

John 10:14–15 NLT

Ever spent much time around sheep? They're really self-centered. All they think about is eating, sleeping, and avoiding conflict. But one good thing about sheep is that they'll drop everything and respond to their shepherd's voice. Not anybody else's voice, just the familiar tones of their own shepherd. This little ewe wants to recognize and respond to her beloved Shepherd's voice, too. How about you, ewe?

Nothing More
than Feelings

LORD, sustain me as you promised,
that I may live!
Do not let my hope be crushed.

PSALM 119:116 NLT

Whatever our foe—unemployment, rejection, loss, illness—we may feel beaten down by life. Hope feels crushed by the relentless boulder bearing down on our souls. We feel that we can't possibly endure another day. Yes, we feel, we feel. But feelings are often deceiving. God promises to sustain us, to strengthen us, so that we might withstand that massive rock. We can trust Him. He will not allow us to be crushed!

Trumped

And the LORD said to Abraham,
"Why did Sarah laugh, saying,
'Shall I indeed bear a child,
when I am so old?' Is anything
too difficult for the LORD?"

GENESIS 18:13–14 NASB

Sarah, well past menopause and losing the
drooping appendage war, was so floored
when told of her impending pregnancy that
she burst into laughter. How absurd to think
those breasts sagging to her navel would
nurse a baby! But that's exactly what God
had in store. We sometimes forget that God
created the systems we consider absolute
and impenetrable. He can trump them all
with a flick of His pinkie!

Forgiveness

Tolerance Isn't Enough

"In his name the nations
will put their hope."

MATTHEW 12:21 NIV

In the summer of 2000, my husband and I toured the Holy Land. Our Israeli guide assured us that there was no safer place than Jerusalem, for people of numerous faiths—Muslim, Jewish, Christian, Hindu— had learned tolerance as the key to living together peaceably. Yet tension was as evident as the armed guards on every street corner. Violence erupted three months later with the first bus bombings. Our only hope for peace is Jehovah.

Redeemed!

O Israel, hope in the LORD; for with
the LORD there is lovingkindness,
and with Him is abundant redemption.

PSALM 130:7 NASB

The psalmist knew Israel had a rotten track
record. Throughout Old Testament history,
God miraculously delivered the Israelites
from trouble repeatedly, and they would
gratefully turn to Him, only to eventually
slip again into rebellion and more trouble.
Sounds a lot like you and me, doesn't it?
But thankfully, ours is a redemptive God;
a God who offers abundant loving-kindness
and forgiveness. A God of second
chances—then and now.

Mr. Clean for the Soul

As far as the east is from the west,
so far has He removed our
transgressions from us.

PSALM 103:12 NASB

Dirty little secrets. We all have them. Exposing them is a popular theme for television shows these days. But we don't have to wallow in the muck of our past. God has promised to wash us clean of our dirty little secrets and remove them as far as the east is from the west when we repent of our wrongdoings and ask him for forgiveness. An immaculate and sparkling fresh start—redemption is Mr. Clean for the soul!

Fresh Start

Questions and Answers

*And the Scriptures were written
to teach and encourage us
by giving us hope.*

ROMANS 15:4 CEV

What do you do when facing a perplexing problem? Ask a family member? Consult a friend? Turn to the Internet?

God's Word is brimming with answers to life's difficulties, yet it's often the last place we turn. God speaks to us today through the lives of trusting Abraham, broken-hearted Ruth, runaway Jonah, courageous Esther, female leader Deborah in a male-dominated society, beaten-down Job, double-crossing Peter, and Paul, who proved people can change.

Hit the Mats

Blessed is he whose help is
the God of Jacob, whose
hope is in the LORD his God.

PSALM 146:5 NIV

Wrestled with God lately? We all do
at one time or another. The Genesis 32
account of Jacob's Almighty wrestling match
reassures us that God is not offended when
we beat on His chest and shout, "Why?"
He understands that we must sometimes
wrestle out the mysteries of our faith.
Wrestling with his Lord was a turning
point for Jacob—he got a new name
(Israel) and a new perspective.
God is ready to do the same
for us.

Friendship

Girlfriends

And our hope for you is firm,
because we know that just
as you share in our sufferings,
so also you share in our comfort.

2 CORINTHIANS 1:7 NIV

Anne of Green Gables was right: Bosom friends are important. Girls need girlfriends. . .little girls and grown-up girls alike. God wired us to need each other, to yearn for the heart-bonding that results from sharing sufferings, comfort, hugs, and giggles. Nothing's wrong with men, of course, but they don't make the same bosom friends as girls. Have you thanked the Lord lately for your soul sisters?

One for All

All of you are part of the same body.
There is only one Spirit of God, just
as you were given one hope when
you were chosen to be God's people.

EPHESIANS 4:4 CEV

Remember the motto of the Three
Musketeers? "All for one and one for all."
Christ-followers should have the same
sense of unity, for we are bound together by
eternal hope, the gift of our Savior. Feeling
with and for each other, we'll cry tears of joy
from one eye and tears of sadness from the
other. Loneliness is not an option. Take the
first step. Reach out today—someone else's
hand is reaching, too.

BFF

I am counting on the LORD;
yes, I am counting on him.
I have put my hope in his word.

PSALM 130:5 NLT

Best Friends Forever" earn this title of
honor because we've learned we can count
on them. They've proven they'll be there
for us through svelte and bloated, sweet and
grumpy, thoughtful and insensitive. Bailing
us out of countless sinking dinghies, they've
held us as we sobbed, fed our families,
watched our kids, and made us smile. How
much more can we count on our Creator to
be there for us?

Future

Heaven's Bakery

*"Those who hope in me
will not be disappointed."*

ISAIAH 49:23 NIV

As I stood in line ogling luscious pastries in the coffee shop's glass case, I asked the teenage clerk which she would suggest. Casting cornflower-blue eyes heavenward, she tapped her dainty chin with one finger before answering in a wistful voice. "I recommend the blueberry cheesecake. When I eat it, I hear angels." What higher recommendation is there? What greater hope have we than heaven? (Maybe they'll even serve blueberry cheesecake there!)

Heading Home

We are only foreigners
living here on earth for a while.

I Chronicles 29:15 CEV

I quivered on the icy Alps peak, more from fear than cold. Which ski slope was my level (beginner) and which were treacherously advanced? A mistake could be deadly. Panic gripped me; I couldn't read the German signs and no one spoke English.

As Christians, we're foreigners on this earth. We don't speak the same language or share the same perspective as nonbelievers. We're only passing through this world on our way to the next. . .heading home.

Beyond the Horizon

Always continue to fear the LORD.
You will be rewarded for this; your
hope will not be disappointed.

PROVERBS 23:17–18 NLT

Have you ever traversed a long, winding road, unable to see your final destination? Perhaps you were surprised by twists and turns along the way or jarred by unexpected potholes. But you were confident that if you stayed on that road, you would eventually reach your destination. Likewise, God has mapped out our futures. The end of the road may disappear beyond the horizon, but we are assured that our destination will not be disappointing.

God's Faithfulness

Never Alone

I am convinced that nothing can ever separate us from God's love. Neither death nor life, neither angels nor demons, neither our fears for today nor our worries about tomorrow—not even the powers of hell can separate us from God's love.

ROMANS 8:38 NLT

I read a poll that said being alone is one of women's worst fears. When we experience loss, we sometimes feel that we're struggling all alone; that others around us can't possibly comprehend the scope of our fears, our worries, our pain. But the Bible says we're not alone, that nothing can separate us from our heavenly Father. He is right there beside us, loving us, offering His companionship when we have none.

I Do

Let us hold unswervingly
to the hope we profess,
for he who promised is faithful.

HEBREWS 10:23 NIV

An important part of any marriage is the vow of faithfulness. We pledge that we will remain faithful to our beloved until death do us part. Faithfulness is crucial to a trusting relationship. We must be able to depend on our spouse to always be in our corner, love us even when we're unlovable, and never leave or forsake us.

God is faithful. We can unswervingly depend on Him to never break His promises.

Can You Hear Me Now?

*But as for me, I watch in hope
for the LORD, I wait for God
my Savior; my God will hear me.*

MICAH 7:7 NIV

If there's anything more frustrating than waiting for someone who never shows, it's trying to talk to someone who isn't listening. It's as if they have plugged their ears and nothing penetrates. Mothers are well acquainted with this exercise in futility, as are wives, daughters, and sisters. But the Bible tells us that God hears us when we talk to Him. He shows up when we wait for Him.

He will not disappoint us.

God's Grace

A New Tomorrow

Rahab the harlot. . .Joshua spared. . .
for she hid the messengers whom
Joshua sent to spy out Jericho.

JOSHUA 6:25 NASB

Rahab was the unlikeliest of heroes: a prostitute who sold her body in the darkest shadows. Yet she was the very person God chose to fulfill His prophecy. How astoundingly freeing! Especially for those of us ashamed of our past. God loved Rahab for who she was—not what she did. Rahab is proof that God can and will use anyone for His higher purposes. Anyone. Even you and me.

83

Pure and Unspoiled

And everyone who has this hope
fixed on Him purifies himself,
just as He is pure.

1 JOHN 3:3 NASB

Don't you just love taking the first scoop of ice cream from a fresh half gallon? There's something about the smooth surface of unspoiled purity that satisfies the soul. It's the same with new jars of peanut butter, freshly fallen snow, or stretches of pristine, early morning beach sand. God looks at us that way—unblemished, pure and unspoiled—through our faith and hope in Him. Allow that thought to bring a smile to your face today.

Unfathomable Grace

Jesus treated us much better
than we deserve. He made us
acceptable to God and gave
us the hope of eternal life.

TITUS 3:7 CEV

Whereas justice is getting what we deserve
and mercy is not getting what we deserve,
grace is getting what we don't deserve.
Thankfully, God doesn't automatically dole
out justice for our myriad sins, but reaches
beyond to mercy and even a step further to
grace. As Jean Valjean discovers in the classic
story, *Les Miserables*, when we truly
grasp God's unfathomable mercy
and grace, we are then em-
powered to extend it to others.

God's Help

The Palm of His Hand

If I ride the wings of the morning, if
I dwell by the farthest oceans, even
there your hand will guide me, and
your strength will support me.

PSALM 139:9–10 NLT

Surf foamed around my ankles as I lifted
the burgundy starfish, its pointed tips curled
in taut contraction. "It's okay little fellow,
I'll help you," I crooned, gently cradling the
sea creature stranded by the outgoing tide.
Tiny tentacles tickled my palm as the starfish
relaxed, safe and protected. Likewise, God's
hand rescues, supports, and guides us to
life-sustaining waters when we're stranded.

We're safe in the palm of His hand.

Roll Down the Window

"Ask and it will be given to you;
seek and you will find; knock
and the door will be opened to you."

LUKE 11:9 NIV

Does your fellow have trouble asking directions? Do you cruise about the country on a scenic tour that could have been avoided by asking a simple question? We all find it difficult to some degree when it comes to asking for help. But that's how we reach our final destinations—and not just on the highway. God offers help if we only ask. He's standing there holding the road map. We just have to stop and roll down the window.

God's Hope

Cherished Desire

God our Father loves us.
He is kind and has given us eternal
comfort and a wonderful hope.

2 THESSALONIANS 2:16 CEV

Webster's definition of hope: "to cherish a desire with expectation." In other words, yearning for something wonderful you expect to occur. Our hope in Christ is not just yearning for something wonderful, as in "I hope for a sunny beach day." It's a deep trust with roots that extend from the beginning of time to the infinite future. Our hope is not just the anticipation of heaven, but the expectation of a fulfilling life walking beside our Creator and best Friend.

Seeking an Oasis

He changes a wilderness
into a pool of water and a
dry land into springs of water.

PSALM 107:35 NASB

The wilderness of Israel is truly a barren
wasteland—nothing but rocks and parched
sand stretching as far as the distant horizon.
The life-and-death contrast between stark
desert and pools of oasis water is startling.
Our lives can feel parched, too. Colorless.
Devoid of life. But God has the power to
transform desert lives into gurgling, spring-
of-water lives. Ask Him to bubble
up springs of hope within you
today.

Name Above All Names

O God, we give glory to you
all day long and constantly
praise your name.

PSALM 44:8 NLT

So what has God done that deserves our everlasting praise? His descriptive names tell the story: A friend that sticks closer than a brother (Proverbs 18:24), Altogether lovely (Song of Solomon 5:16), The rock that is higher than I (Psalm 61:2), My strength and my song (Isaiah 12:2), The lifter of my head (Psalm 3:3), Shade from the heat (Isaiah 25:4). His very name fills us with hope!

First Love

But you must stay deeply rooted and firm in your faith. You must not give up the hope you received when you heard the good news.

COLOSSIANS 1:23 CEV

Do you remember the day you turned your life over to Christ? Can you recall the flood of joy and hope that coursed through your veins? Ah, the wonder of first love. Like romantic love that deepens and broadens with passing years, our relationship with Jesus evolves into a river of faith that endures the test of time.

Feel the Love

Long before he laid down earth's
foundations, he had us in mind,
had settled on us as the focus of
his love, to be made whole
and holy by his love.

EPHESIANS 1:4 MSG

Need a boost of hope today? Read this
passage aloud, inserting your name for each
"us." Wow! Doesn't that bring home the
message of God's incredible, extravagant,
customized love for you? I am the focus of
His love, and I bask in the hope of healing,
wholeness, and holiness His individualized
attention brings. You too, dear sister, are
His focus. Allow yourself to feel the love
today.

Forever and Always

"Never will I leave you;
never will I forsake you."
HEBREWS 13:5 NIV

Unconditional love. We all yearn for it—from our parents, our spouses, our children, our friends. Love not based on our performance or accomplishments, but on who we are deep down beneath the fluff. God promises unconditional love to those who honor Him. We don't need to worry about disappointing Him when He gets to know us better—He knows us already. Better than we know ourselves. And He loves us anyway, forever and always.

God's Sovereignty

Astounding Rescue

*Then I remember something
that fills me with hope.
The Lord's kindness never fails!*

LAMENTATIONS 3:21–22 CEV

With our hectic lifestyles, pausing to
remember the past isn't something we do
very often. But perhaps we should. Then
when doubts assault our faith, fears threaten
to devour us and disaster hovers like a dark
cloud, we'll remember God's past loving-
kindnesses. Hope will triumph over despair.
Keeping a prayer journal is a wonderful way
to chronicle answered prayer. We'll always
remember the times when God's
merciful hands rescued us in
astounding ways.

Keeping Us in Stitches

The secret things belong
to the LORD our God.
DEUTERONOMY 29:29 NIV

Have you ever noticed the messy underside of a needlepoint picture? Ugly knots, loose threads, and clashing colors appear random, without pattern. Yet if you turn it over, an exquisite intricate design is revealed, each stitch blending to create a beautiful finished picture. Such is the fabric of our lives. The knots and loose threads may not make sense to us, but the Master Designer has a plan. The secret design belongs to Him.

Large and In Charge

"In this world you will have trouble.
But take heart!
I have overcome the world."

JOHN 16:33 NIV

"Who's in charge here?" Most mothers have had the experience of returning home to a chaos-wrecked house. Toys, books, clothes, snack wrappers everywhere. "Why isn't [insert correct answer here: your father, the babysitter, Grandma, etc.] in control?"

Our world can sometimes feel chaotic like that. Things appear to be spinning out of control. But we must remember that God is large and in charge. He has a plan.

God's Word

One Hunky Verse

To Him who is able to do
far more abundantly beyond
all that we ask or think,
according to the power that
works within us, to Him be the
glory. . .forever and ever. Amen.

EPHESIANS 3:20–21 NASB

Don't you just love the bigness of this verse? It radiates with the enormity of God—that nothing is beyond His scope or power. Read it aloud and savor the words far more abundantly. Now repeat "beyond all that we ask or think" three times, pondering each word individually. Wow! If there was ever a hunky verse to cast an attitude of gratitude over our day, this is it. Yay God!

Only the Best

I have hidden your word in my heart, that I might not sin against you.

PSALM 119:11 NLT

I adore homemade chicken salad. Honey mustard, sliced grapes, and slivered almonds make it delicious. Quality ingredients produce quality results. It's all poultry, but there's a big difference between white meat and gizzards.

Memorizing scripture is like preparing chicken salad for the soul. God's Word (quality ingredients) will be ready at a moment's notice to guide, comfort, and train us in righteousness (quality results).

Anything else is just gizzards.

A Lifetime Award

O Lord, you alone are my hope.
I've trusted you, O LORD,
from childhood.

PSALM 71:5 NLT

My heart swelled like an over-inflated balloon. Tears blurred my vision as little Josh bounded for the stage, his blond cowlick flopping in the breeze. As his second grade Sunday school teacher, I had worked tirelessly to help him memorize ten Bible verses. Josh beamed at the shiny medal encircling his neck, but I knew that his true reward was God's Word implanted in his heart to guide him for the rest of his life.

Healing

Permission to Mourn

When I heard this, I sat down
and cried. Then for several days,
I mourned; I went without eating
to show my sorrow, and I prayed.

NEHEMIAH 1:4 CEV

Bad news. When it arrives, what's your reaction? Do you scream? Fall apart? Run away? Nehemiah's response to bad news is a model for us. First, he vented his sorrow. It's okay to cry and mourn. Christians suffer pain like everyone else—only we know the source of inner healing. Disguising our struggle doesn't make us look more spiritual. . . just less real. Like Nehemiah, our next step is to turn to the only true source of help and comfort.

Healing Heat

When I am weak,
then I am strong.

2 Corinthians 12:10 nasb

As an occupational therapist, I make splints for people with broken bones. The thermoplastic splinting material comes in sheets, hard and unyielding as plywood. When heated, the thermoplastic becomes pliable so it can be cut and molded into a form that promotes healing.

Like that thermoplastic, we're strongest and most usable when we've gone through the melting process. Heat transforms us into moldable beings with which God heals hearts and spirits.

Pebbles

"I will give you a new heart and put
a new spirit within you; and I will
remove the heart of stone from your
flesh and give you a heart of flesh."

EZEKIEL 36:26 NASB

So many things can harden our hearts:
overwhelming loss; shattered dreams;
even scar tissue from broken hearts,
disillusionment, and disappointment. To
avoid pain, we simply turn off feelings. Our
hearts become petrified rock—heavy, cold,
and rigid. But God can crack our hearts of
stone from the inside out and replace that
miserable pile of pebbles with soft, feeling
hearts of flesh. The amazing result is
a brand new, hope-filled spirit.

Do a Little Dance

Then Miriam. . .took a tambourine
and led all the women as they played
their tambourines and danced.

EXODUS 15:20 NLT

Can you imagine the enormous celebration
that broke out among the children of Israel
when God miraculously saved them from
Pharaoh's army? Even dignified prophetess
Miriam grabbed her tambourine and cut
loose with her girlfriends. Despite adverse
circumstances, she heard God's music and did
His dance. Isn't that our goal today? To Hear
God's music above the world's cacophony
and do His dance as we recognize everyday miracles in our lives?

Did You Say
Something?

"Call to Me and I will answer you,
and I will tell you great and mighty
things, which you do not know."

As someone who's been there, done that, you've gotta love the commercial where the husband has his face buried in the newspaper when his wife pops the no-win question: "Does this dress make me look fat?" "You bet," he distractedly replies.

God promises to not only hear us when we call to Him, but to answer by teaching us new and amazing things. He's never distracted. He's always listening. And He always cares.

Heaven

Payday

"Go into all the world and
preach the gospel to all creation."

MARK 16:15 NASB

One day as our family discussed the Great
Commission over dinner, my salesman
husband asked my young daughter if she
knew what commission meant. "Sure," she
replied. "It's what you get paid at the end for
what you did in the beginning."

Our commission will be paid in heaven
when we're surrounded not only by dear
friends and family with whom we shared
our faith, but also the souls reached
by missions we supported with
our time, money, and energies.

It's Not Over

When the wicked die,
their hopes die with them,
for they rely on their
own feeble strength.

PROVERBS 11:7 NLT

Tony Dungy, Super Bowl champion, coach, and author of *Quiet Strength*, said, "It's because of God's goodness that we can have hope, both for here and the hereafter." Coach Dungy's testimony of eternal hope for those who rely on God's infinite strength touched many hearts after the tragic loss of his teenage son. Death is not the end. There is a hope, a future for those who choose to not rely on their own feeble strength.

Streets of Treats

What you hope for is kept
safe for you in heaven.

COLOSSIANS 1:5 CEV

Heaven. Will the streets really be paved
with gold? Or even better—chocolate?
No, if our earthly treasures are our source
of security and hope, we're in trouble.
Rust, thieves, decay, recession. . .things
just aren't safe. But peace? Joy? Reveling
forever in our Lord's presence? All waiting
for us safely in heaven. (But who says we
can't hope for Godiva-cobbled streets?)

Joy

Soul Sister

"I always see the Lord near me, and I will not be afraid with him at my right side. Because of this, my heart will be glad, my words will be joyful, and I will live in hope."

ACTS 2:25–26 CEV

Laughter is the soul sister of joy; they often travel together. Humor is the primary catalyst for releasing joy into our souls and making our hearts glad. It's healthy for us, too! Laughter is cleansing and healing, a powerful salve for the wounds of life. . .a natural medicine and tremendous stress reliever. Laughing is to joy what a 50 percent off sign is to shopping. It motivates us to seek more, more, more!

Smiling Hearts

Weeping may last for the night,
but a shout of joy comes in
the morning.

PSALM 30:5 NASB

What woman hasn't seen the dim
underbelly of 2 a.m. through hot tears? God
gave us emotionally sensitive spirits and is
willing to sit with us as we weep through the
long, hard night. Sometimes "night" lasts
for a season. But He promises that the sun
will eventually rise. And on that glorious
morning, we'll be filled with so much joy,
even our hearts will smile. Joy is
appreciated most in the wake
of disappointment.

JOY: Jesus Occupying You

May all who fear you find
in me a cause for joy,
for I have put my hope in your word.

PSALM 119:74 NLT

Have you ever met someone you immediately knew was filled with joy? The kind of effervescent joy that bubbles up and overflows, covering everyone around her with warmth and love and acceptance. We love to be near people filled with Jesus-joy. And even more, as Christians we want to be like them! Lord, remind us how:

> J—Jesus
> O—Occupying
> Y—You

Justice

Justice for All?

*Our God, you save us,
and your fearsome deeds answer
our prayers for justice!*

PSALM 65:5 CEV

It's not fair! How many times have we
uttered this indignant cry when life handed
us injustice? We demand justice—it's what
we deserve, right? But what about all those
times we've misstepped or misjudged?
James 2:13 tells us that mercy triumphs
over justice. Mercy forgives mistakes and
doesn't dole out what is deserved. Mercy—
like a jail sentence pardoned. Mercy—
like a man on a cross.

As the Tide Turns

"He will not falter or be discouraged
till he establishes justice on earth.
In his law the islands will
put their hope."

ISAIAH 42:4 NIV

Change. . .besides our unalterable Lord,
it's the only thing constant in this world. Yet
the only person who likes change is a baby
with a wet diaper. Isaiah prophesied that the
Almighty will one day create positive change
on earth. Like the tides that clean beach
debris after a storm, positive change washes
away the old and refreshes with the new.
In this we hope.

Knowing God

Up is the Only Out

Let them lie face down in the dust,
for there may be hope at last.
LAMENTATIONS 3:29 NLT

The Old Testament custom for grieving people was to lie prostrate and cover themselves with ashes. Perhaps the thought was that when you're wallowing in the dust, at least you can't descend any further. There's an element of hope in knowing that there's only one way to go: up. If a recent loss has you sprawled in the dust, know that God doesn't waste pain in our lives. He will use it for some redeeming purpose.

Welcome Back

Train up a child in the way he
should go: and when he is old,
he will not depart from it.

PROVERBS 22:6 KJV

I'll never forget the tender bedtime family gatherings on my sister's bed when I was a child. After reading a Bible story from the big picture Bible, we took turns praying. When I had children, I established the same tradition in our home. The Bible promises that if we instill God's Word and principles in our children, they will one day return to it. It may take time, but God's Word will not return void.

Who's Your Daddy?

His name is the LORD. . . .
A father to the fatherless.

PSALM 68:4–5 NIV

His father left when my friend Ben was two. Ben recognized him once—from pictures—at a family funeral, but his father intentionally turned away. When Ben was 35, with a family of his own, his father suddenly showed up, seeking a relationship. Sadly, he was diagnosed with cancer shortly after their reunion and died within one year. Ben mourned but knew his real paternal relationship was with God, the Father to the fatherless.

Learning

Live and Learn

Lead me by your truth and teach me,
for you are the God who saves me.
All day long I put my hope in you.

PSALM 25:5 NLT

Acquiring spiritual wisdom is a fluid
process. Trickles pool into mighty reservoirs
from which we draw hope. God is right
beside us moment by moment, day by
day, guiding us, teaching us, feeding our
reservoirs. But if we freeze the Holy Spirit
out of our lives by apathetic or indifferent
attitudes, the trickle solidifies into ice and
the flow of wisdom is blocked. If we keep our
minds open to God's everyday lessons, just
watch the river surge!

Getting to Know You

*For the law never made
anything perfect. But now we have
confidence in a better hope,
through which we draw near to God.*

HEBREWS 7:19 NLT

Following Old Testament law used to be
considered the way to achieve righteousness,
but obeying rules just doesn't work for fallible
humans. We mess up. We fail miserably. Then
Jesus came and provided a better way to draw
near to God. He bridged the gap by offering
us a personal relationship rather than rules.
Together we laugh, cry, love, grieve,
rejoice. We get to know our Papa
God through our personal
relationship with Him.

Fresh and Green

They will still bear fruit in old age,
they will stay fresh and green.

PSALM 92:14 NIV

Doris, a tiny 90-year-old widow in my Bible study, is teaching me how to be a blessing. That's her prayer every morning of her life: Lord, make me a blessing to someone today. And sure enough, God uses her to touch lives in His name—helping a frantic woman find her lost keys; taking a sick neighbor to the doctor; offering a friendly word to the grumpy, wheelchair-bound man. Little blessings are big indeed to those in need.

Rocky Road

But by faith we eagerly await through the Spirit the righteousness for which we hope.

GALATIANS 5:5 NIV

My daughter's five-pound Russian Terror (oops—that's Terrier) is anything but righteous. Rocky dashes after cars, nibbles poisonous plants, and routinely ingests ripped-apart rugs. In order to guide said pup along the path of righteousness, doors must close. Our paths of righteousness are also guided by the One who shuts doors according to what's best for us. So, girlfriends—enough howling, whining, and scratching at closed doors!

Not Suzie
Homemaker

The Spirit has given each of us
a special way of serving others.

1 CORINTHIANS 12:7 CEV

My friend Denise has the gift of
hospitality. She welcomes people into her
home and makes them feel loved through
her thoughtful accents: serving food on
her best china, lighting scented candles,
offering cozy furnishings. Hospitality is
not my gift. My guests get bagged chips,
flat soda, and leave coated in cat hair. God
taught me not to compare and despair, for
He has given each of us our own gift to be
used for His service. What's yours?

Lifestyle

Superwoman Isn't Home

"But we will devote ourselves to prayer and to the ministry of the word."

ACTS 6:4 NASB

As busy women, we've found out the hard way that we can't do everything. Heaven knows we've tried, but the truth has found us out: Superwoman is a myth. So we must make priorities and focus on the most important. Prayer and God's Word should be our faith priorities. If we only do as much as we can do, then God will take over and do what only He can do. He's got our backs, girls!

Walkin' Boots

I heard about you from others;
now I have seen you
with my own eyes.

JOB 42:5 CEV

As children we sang, "Jesus loves me, this I know; for the Bible tells me so," and we believed because, well, we were told to. But we reach a crossroads as adults: Either pull on the boots of faith and take ownership or simply polish them occasionally—maybe at Easter and Christmas—and allow them to sit neglected and dusty in the closet. Have you taken ownership of your faith? Go ahead, sister, those boots were made for walkin'!

Working Out

I will never give up
hope or stop praising you.
PSALM 71:14 CEV

Praise is like a muscle; if we don't exercise it regularly, it becomes weak and atrophied. But if we flex and extend an attitude of gratitude daily, praise grows into a strong, dependable force that nurtures hope and carries us through the worst of circumstances. Like Helen Keller, though blind and deaf, we'll praise our Creator: "I thank God for my handicaps, for through them, I have found myself, my work, and my God."

Living Joyfully

Inexplicable Strength

"The joy of the LORD is your strength."
NEHEMIAH 8:10 NASB

Joy is not based on the circumstances around us. It is not synonymous with happiness. God promised believers His deep, abiding joy—not fleeting happiness, which is here today, gone tomorrow. The joy of the Lord rises above external situations and supernaturally overshadows everything else to become our inexplicable, internal strength.

He is Able

The prospect of the righteous is joy.

PROVERBS 10:28 NIV

Living joyfully isn't denying reality. The righteous do not receive a "Get Out of Pain Free" card when they place their trust in Christ. We all have hurts in our lives. Some we think we cannot possibly endure. But even in the midst of our darkest times, our heavenly Father is able to reach in with gentle fingers to touch us and infuse us with joy that defies explanation. Impossible? Perhaps by the world's standards. Yet He is able.

Forever Joy

We don't look at the troubles
we can see now. . . . For the things we
see now will soon be gone, but the
things we cannot see will last forever.

2 CORINTHIANS 4:18 NLT

A painter's first brush strokes look like
random blobs—no discernable shape,
substance, or clue as to what the completed
painting will be. But in time, the skilled
artist brings order to perceived chaos.
Initial confusion is forgotten in joyful
admiration of the finished masterpiece.

We often can't see past the blobs of
trouble on our life canvases. We must trust
that the Artist has a masterpiece
underway. And there will be great
joy in its completion.

Perfect Love

Love never gives up, never loses faith, is always hopeful, and endures through every circumstance.

1 CORINTHIANS 13:7 NLT

We have relationships in three directions: upward (with God), outward (with others), and inward (with ourselves). We are bound to be disappointed at one time or another by the latter two. Because of human frailty, we will inevitably experience failure by others and even ourselves. Our imperfect love will be strained to the breaking point. But our Creator will never fail us—His perfect love never gives up on us.

Lighthouse Love

For God, who said, "Light shall shine out of darkness," is the One who has shone in our hearts.

2 CORINTHIANS 4:6 NASB

Have you heard the story of the lighthouse keeper's daughter who kept faithful vigil for her sailor? Every night she watched as the light's beam pierced the blackness and sliced through raging storms, driven by relentless hope that her lover would return to her on the morning's tide. God loves us like that. He's our light in the darkness: guiding, beckoning, and filling our hearts with hope. He never tires. He never stops.

Three Little Words

Three things will last
forever—faith, hope, and love.

1 CORINTHIANS 13:13 NLT

Don't you get tired of throwing away panty hose? It's hard to believe that modern technology can scan quivers inside our livers and detect nickel-sized puddles on Mars, but we still can't manufacture hose that won't run. Yep, there are precious few things that endure. Only three, the Bible says: faith, hope, and love. Three things that will never break down, wear out, or get lost. These are the only things worth keeping.

New Life

New Life

God is so good, and by raising
Jesus from death, he has given us
new life and a hope that lives on.

1 PETER 1:3 CEV

The words of a song I wrote while pregnant
with my first child exult in the similarities
between new physical life and fresh spiritual
life in Christ: "New life stirs within me now.
Like a soft breeze, transforming me now. It's
a miracle of love, precious blessing from
above. My heart has taken wings. . .lift me up!"

New life. By the goodness of God, we can
experience this precious transformation no
less miraculous than a baby growing within us.

Time-out

"The LORD will not abandon
His people."

1 SAMUEL 12:22 NASB

Do you remember when, as a little girl, you languished alone in your room as punishment? Or maybe you sat with your nose plastered to the corner in time-out. It felt like your parents had abandoned you, didn't it? As adults, we sometimes feel abandoned when that's not the case at all. We're actually in a place strategically chosen by a loving Father to teach us, broaden us, and improve us in the end.

That Morning

You have placed your faith and hope
in God because he raised Christ from
the dead and gave him great glory.

1 PETER 1:21 NLT

Have you ever wondered how Mary felt that
Easter morning when she discovered Jesus'
tomb empty? Already grieving, imagine
the shock of discovering the body of her
Savior—the One who held all her hopes and
dreams—gone! How can that be? Maybe. . . ?
Hope glimmers. But no—impossible. He
did say something about resurrection, but
that was figurative, wasn't it? Who are. . .You
are? I must run and tell them. It's true! He
has risen! He's alive! My hope lives, too!

Patience

Patience of Hope

We call to mind your work
of faith, your labor of love,
and your patience of hope
in following our Master,
Jesus Christ, before God our Father.

1 THESSALONIANS 1:3 MSG

Labor. The word alone draws a shudder
from the most stalwart of pregnant women.
Just as laboring to bring forth new physical
life requires patience, birthing new spiritual
life may require an intensive labor of love:
ceaseless prayer. Countless women on their
knees praying for the salvation of
a loved one have rejoiced in
answered prayer. Their secret?
Patience of hope.

Bigger and Better

Waiting does not diminish us,
any more than waiting diminishes a
pregnant mother. . . . The longer we
wait, . . .the more joyful our expectancy.

ROMANS 8:24–25 MSG

Life is filled with waiting—on slow people,
transportation, doctor reports, even for God
to act. Waiting often requires patience we
don't have. It feels like perpetual pregnancy—
anticipating a baby that is never delivered.
The secret is to clasp hands with our Lord.
He offers His shield of protection from impatience, irritability, and anger and replaces
them with self-control, kindness, and joy.

Waiting is inevitable, but we can
draw closer to the Father in the
waiting.

Wait Just a Minute

We wait in hope for the LORD;
he is our help and our shield.

PSALM 33:20 NIV

Impatience: archenemy of women. Like Batman's Riddler, or Superman's Lex Luthor, impatience stalks us, plots our demise, and blindsides us via thoughtless neighbors, inconsiderate drivers, careless clerks, dense husbands, children taking for–ev–er. But waiting is an unavoidable part of life, and the Bible says we don't have to be undone by it. The Lord's patience is our shield and defense, and He's got plenty stockpiled.

Peace

Please Rescue Me

I long for you to rescue me!
Your word is my only hope.

PSALM 119:81 CEV

Have you ever longed to be rescued? Stranded after shredding knee ligaments during a remote mountain skiing accident, I waited helplessly for rescuers to arrive. All alone on the raw Canadian mountainside, I felt fear mount. Freezing temperatures, prowling cougars, and unrelenting pain threatened to engulf me in despair. So I did the most and the least I could do: I prayed and recited scripture. And my faithful heavenly Father rescued me with His peace.

Guilt-Free

"I will forgive their wickedness,
and I will never again
remember their sins."

HEBREWS 8:12 NLT

Guilt. It tends to consume us women to the
point that ninety percent of the things we do
are motivated by guilt. But God says we don't
have to allow guilt to control us. We should
learn from past mistakes, certainly, and
then shed the guilt like a moth-eaten winter
coat. Don a fresh spring outfit and look
ahead. Our past prepares us for the future if
we are open to the present.

Climb In

May the God of hope fill you
with all joy and peace as you trust
in him, so that you may overflow with
hope by the power of the Holy Spirit.

ROMANS 15:13 NIV

Trust is the bottom line when it comes
to living an abundant life. We will never
escape the muddy ruts without trusting that
God has the leverage and power to pull us
out of the quagmire. They say faith is like
believing the tight rope walker can cross
the gorge pushing a wheelbarrow. Trust is
climbing into his wheelbarrow. Only when
we climb into God's wheelbarrow can His
joy and peace overflow as hope into
our hearts.

Hope Resurrected

We had hoped that he would be the one to set Israel free! But it has already been three days since all this happened.

LUKE 24:21 CEV

The scenario for this scripture is quite unusual. Two of Jesus' disciples are describing their lost hope due to the events surrounding Jesus' death to none other than Jesus Himself. They don't recognize Him as they walk together on the road to Emmaus after His resurrection. Spiritual cataracts blind them to the hope they thought was dead—right in front of them! Let's open our spiritual eyes to Jesus, who is walking beside us.

Sprouts

"For there is hope for a tree,
when it is cut down,
that it will sprout again."

JOB 14:7 NASB

Have you ever battled a stubborn tree? You
know, one you can saw off at the ground but
the tenacious thing keeps sprouting new
growth from the roots? You have to admire
the resiliency of that life force, struggling
in its refusal to give up. That's hope in a
nutshell, sisters. We must believe, even
as stumps, that we will eventually become
majestic, towering evergreens if we just
keep sending out those sprouts.

Counting on It

Blessed is the man who
perseveres under trial, because
when he has stood the test,
he will receive the crown
of life that God has promised
to those who love him.

JAMES 1:12 NIV

Some think that when you turn your life
over to Christ, troubles are over. But if
you've been a believer for more than a
day, you'll realize that the Christian life is
no Caribbean cruise. There will be trials;
there will be tribulations. Count on it. But
Jesus promises a glorious reward for our
perseverance through those
hard times. Count on that
even more.

Power

Sprung

*I will free your prisoners from
death in a waterless dungeon.
Come back to the place of safety,
all you prisoners who still have hope!*

ZECHARIAH 9:11–12 NLT

In the marvelous book, *The Count of
Monte Cristo*, Edmond Dantes is unjustly
imprisoned. Against all odds, God enables
him to escape and eventually return
victorious, a hope-filled man.

Have you ever felt trapped in a prison of
hopelessness? Financial difficulties, poor
health, unemployment, rocky marriage,
delinquent children—there are countless
dungeons that shackle us. But God
promises hope and freedom from
our prisons. Jesus bailed us out!

Overflowing Love

Precious in the sight of the LORD
is the death of His godly ones.

PSALM 116:15 NASB

Jesus wept. Two small words that portray the enormity of Jesus' emotion following the death of His dear friend, Lazarus (John 11:35). Jesus knew Lazarus wouldn't stay dead, that he'd soon miraculously rise from the grave. So why did Jesus weep? The depth of His love for those precious to Him overflowed. Our Lord grieves with us in our losses today and comforts us with the knowledge that His beloved will rise to eternal life in heaven.

Power Source

*He gives strength to the weary
and increases the power of the weak.*

ISAIAH 40:29 NIV

Sometimes we feel as if our backs will break under the burdens we carry: debt, responsibilities, impossible schedules. But our God promises to strengthen and empower us if we turn to Him for help. He knows. He cares. He is able.

It's been written that persecuted European Christians don't pray for God to lessen their loads like American Christians do. Instead, they pray for stronger backs.

Prayer

No Call-Waiting

"Call upon me and come
and pray to me,
and I will listen to you."

JEREMIAH 29:12 NIV

"I will listen to you." Every woman's dream.

Jeremiah knew the importance of being listened to. He proclaimed God's message for forty years to the unseeing, unhearing, unresponsive nation of Judah. His ironic good news: God is listening!

Do you ever feel like no one's listening? The Bible says God hears us every time we utter His name. How precious we are to our Creator that He bends His omnipotent ear each time we call on Him.

Juiced

God is our refuge and strength,
a very present help in trouble.

PSALM 46:1 NASB

Remember the scene from the movie *Air Force One*, when Harrison Ford, as the U.S. President, calls for help from the belly of a terrorist-hijacked plane after much death-defying effort? Just as the crucial call is dialed, his cell phone battery conks out. Can you identify? What a relief that our direct line to God—prayer—is always juiced and never needs recharging!

Close to You

I stay close to you,
and your powerful arm supports me.

PSALM 63:8 CEV

There's an old saying: "I used to be close to God, but someone moved." If God is the same yesterday, today, and tomorrow, He's not the one going anywhere. So how do we stay close to God? So close that His powerful arm supports, protects, and lifts us up when we're down? Prayer: as a lifestyle, as much a part of ourselves as breathing. Prayer isn't just spiritual punctuation; it's every word of our life story.

Priorities

Slip-Sliding Away

Instruct those who are rich. . .to fix
their hope on the uncertainty
of riches, but on God, who richly
supplies us with all things to enjoy.

1 TIMOTHY 6:17 NASB

My friend Claire lived large with a
millionaire husband, enormous house,
designer clothes, and flashy convertible—
even a cook (to my envy!). But suddenly the
economy headed south, and in the twinkle
of a bank vault key, she lost it all. Divorced,
homeless, and bitter, Claire was forced to
wait tables to pay her ill son's medical bills.
We can't depend on money—here today,
gone tomorrow. Our hope must be fixed on
our eternal God.

Daily Duties

Let all that you do
be done in love.

1 CORINTHIANS 16:14 NASB

Sometimes we get so wrapped up in our
daily to-do lists that we put our duties above
people. "Leave me alone until this project is
finished, kids." "Sorry, Sue, I'm too busy to
have lunch." "Oh, I don't have time to talk to
Mom today; I'll let the answering machine
get it."

How, then, can we ever share the love
of Christ with those we've shoved out of our
way? People don't care how much
you know until they know how
much you care.

One Nation under God

The poor are filled with hope,
and injustice is silenced.

JOB 5:16 CEV

"Give me your tired, your poor, your huddled masses. . . ." beckons the Statue of Liberty, offering a home and freedom to hurting people. Many of our ancestors flocked to American shores that were offering freedom of worship and an end to the injustice of religious persecution. May we never forget the sacrifices they made to pursue the hope of providing their children—you and me—with a nation founded on Christian principles. Let's strive to preserve that hope for future generations.

A Strong Tower

The name of the LORD is a strong tower;
the righteous run to it and are safe.

PROVERBS 18:10 NIV

We of the twenty-first century tend to limit our references to God, but ancient Hebrew translations offer a broader perspective. There is intrinsic hope in the names of God: *Elohim* (Mighty Creator), *El Olam* (The Everlasting God), *Yahweh Yireh* (The Lord Will Provide), *Yahweh Shalom* (The Lord Is Peace), *Yawheh Tsuri* (The Lord, My Rock), and *Abba* (Father) to name a few. Let's broaden our scope of His powerful name in our prayers today.

24/7

He will not allow your foot to slip—
he who watches over you
will not slumber.

PSALM 121:3 NIV

I love hiking the winding mountain paths near our remote Smoky Mountain cabin. Sometimes I get so caught up in watching hummingbirds or admiring cliff-side vistas that I stumble, forgetting that inattention could be deadly. How comforting to know that our Lord is always alert as He watches over us. We don't have to worry that an important prayer will slip by while He sneezes or that He'll nap through our surgery. He's always on duty.

Papa God

And he did it, rescued us from certain doom. And he'll do it again, rescuing us as many times as we need rescuing.

2 CORINTHIANS 1:10 MSG

"Don't touch!" Lauren scolded her toddler who was reaching for the electrical cord. "No!" Lauren grabbed the nickel from little Erin's hand as it headed toward her mouth. "Always hold Mommy's hand!" Lauren reminded Erin as she dashed for the street. Mothers repeatedly rescue children from dangers they can't comprehend. Likewise, our heavenly Father rescues us from unforeseen consequences. Breathe a grateful prayer today.

Provision

One Gutsy Gal

"It could be that you were made
queen for a time like this!"

ESTHER 4:14 CEV

Crowned queen after winning a beauty
contest, Esther was only allowed audience
with her king when summoned. A wave
of his scepter would pardon her from
execution, but he was a hard man—and
unpredictable. When Esther learned of
a plot to destroy her people, she faced a
tough decision. She was the only one who
could save them—at supreme risk. God had
intentionally placed her in that position for
that time. What's your divinely
ordained position?

Cool Summer Shower

He will renew your life and sustain you in your old age.

RUTH 4:15 NIV

Ruth's blessing of renewal is applicable to us today. *Renovatio* is Latin for "rebirth." It means casting off the old and embracing the new: a revival of spirit, a renovation of attitude. Something essential for women to espouse every day of their lives. Like a cool rain shower on a sizzling summer day, Ruth's hope was renewed by her Lord's touch, and ours will be, too, if we look to Him for daily replenishing.

Raising Our Hopes

"Did I ask you for a son, my lord?"
she said. "Didn't I tell you,
'Don't raise my hopes'?"

2 KINGS 4:28 NIV

Are you afraid to raise your hope in God's provision for fear that hope will crash and burn? The woman from Shunem had everything but her heart's desire—a child. She was afraid to believe Elisha's prediction of her pregnancy but his prayerful intervention made her dream come true. When the boy later died, however, she lashed out. God restored her son and raised her hope from the dead. Literally. Dare we raise our hopes, too?

Refreshment

Zombie Zone

Be joyful in hope,
patient in affliction,
faithful in prayer.

ROMANS 12:12 NIV

Affliction has a tendency to suck the joy right out of our lives, leaving us stranded in the dully-funks. You know—that black hole of existence where our minds fog, emotions go numb, eyes glaze over, and we languish in a state of spiritual dullness. A spiritual zombie zone. But if we're faithful in prayer, God will be faithful to rescue us from those joy-sucking dully-funks and fill us to the brim with His abundant joy.

Divine Refreshment

"You were tired out by the length
of your road, yet you did not say,
'It is hopeless.' You found renewed
strength, therefore you did not faint."

ISAIAH 57:10 NASB

By the end of each day, most women are
ready to collapse. Tight schedules, relentless
deadlines, and plaguing debts make our
daily roads not just physically tiring but
spiritually draining. How encouraging to
know that renewed strength is available
through the fountain that never runs dry. If
we fill our buckets with living water—Bible
reading, Christian music, inspirational
books and DVDs—we will not faint,
but enjoy divine refreshment.

Nonstick Attitudes

A joyful heart is good medicine.
PROVERBS 17:22 NASB

Laughter is to hope as nonstick cooking spray is to a shiny new muffin tin: It keeps the goo from sticking. Once the batter of everyday responsibility hardens and adheres to our attitudes, it's awfully hard to scrape off enough crust for hope to shine through. But if we coat our day with a little laughter and the joy of the Lord, problems will slide off a lot better. And hope sparkles.

Relationships

Two-Stranded Rope

The widow who is really in need and
left all alone puts her hope in God
and continues night and day to pray
and to ask God for help.

1 TIMOTHY 5:5 NIV

Some women feel as though they are irreparably weakened when they are widowed. Where there once were three strands of a sturdy rope (his, hers, and God's), there now are two. But those who persevere through faith and true grit say the secret is to learn to rejoice in what's left instead of lamenting what has been lost. Look forward. Move forward. Keep that two-stranded rope strong, and never lose hope of a better tomorrow.

Glimmering Gold

So in everything, do to others
what you would have
them do to you.

MATTHEW 7:12 NIV

The Golden Rule. Most of us were raised
with this basic guide to human relations, but
sometimes the message gets turned around.
Instead, we follow the Nedlog (golden
backward) Rule: Don't do for others because
they don't do for you. But Jesus didn't say
repay in kind; He said pay forward. The
actions of others are irrelevant. Regardless
of what others do, we should treat
them the way we'd like to be
treated: with respect and
consideration.

Bet the Farm

When the plowman plows
and the thresher threshes,
they ought to do so in the
hope of sharing in the harvest.

1 CORINTHIANS 9:10 NIV

There's a young man who works in children's church with me who is loud, brash, impulsive, an incessant talker, and loves the Lord with all his heart. The kids think he's hilarious. I think he's obnoxious. But I must remind myself that God uses him in unique ways to reach young hearts with the gospel that I never could. He's a plowman and I'm a thresher, and we work together to harvest souls into God's kingdom.

The Salvage Master

*We are pressed on every side
by troubles, but we are not crushed.*

2 CORINTHIANS 4:8 NLT

Many women struggle with depression at some point in their lives: post-partum, kids-partum (empty nest), brain-partum (menopause), and anytime in between. We feel that we are being compressed into a rock-hard cube like the product of a trash compactor. The normal details of life suddenly become perplexing and overwhelming. But God does not abandon us to the garbage dump. He is the Salvage Master and recycles us into sterling images of His glory.

Makeover

Since I was worse than anyone else,
God had mercy on me and let me
be an example of the endless
patience of Christ Jesus.

1 TIMOTHY 1:16 CEV

Saul was a Jesus-hater. He went out of his way to hunt down believers to torture, imprison, and kill. Yet Christ tracked him down and confronted him in a blinding light on a dusty road. Saul's past no longer mattered. Previous sins were forgiven and forgotten. He was given a fresh start. A life makeover. We, too, are offered a life makeover. Christ offers to create a beautiful new image of Himself in us, unblemished and wrinkle-free.

Wings

This means that anyone who belongs to Christ has become a new person. The old life is gone; a new life has begun!

2 CORINTHIANS 5:17 NLT

Have you ever seen a butterfly crawling on her belly with caterpillars? Or trying desperately to hang on to her cocoon as she takes to the skies? Of course not—she spreads her wings and flies far away from her old life, discovering new and wonderful things she never knew existed.

New life in Christ is full of discoveries and wonders, but you can't get there if you're still clutching the old life. It's time to let go, sister.

Rest

Look to the Sunrise

I rise before dawn and cry for help;
I have put my hope in your word.

PSALM 119:147 NIV

Could be stress or worry or berserk
hormones. Whatever the cause, many
women find themselves staring at their dark
bedroom ceilings in the wee morning hours.
We try counting sheep, but they morph
into naughty little children, and we exhaust
ourselves chasing them through fitful
dreams. We're tormented by the "what if's,"
guilted by the "should have's," and jolted
wider awake by the "don't forget to's." But a
new day is dawning and help is but
a prayer away.

Desert Oasis

Find rest, O my soul, in God alone;
my hope comes from him.

PSALM 62:5 NIV

Rest. Far too elusive in our world
of bustling busyness. Overwhelming
responsibilities run us ragged. We find
ourselves not just physically frazzled,
but bankrupt of spirit. Exhaustion steals
our joy.

Like an oasis in the desert, our Father
offers rest for our weary souls and restores
our hope. He helps us unload our burdens,
relax beside His still waters, and drink in
the sparkling refreshment of truth.

Chill

I lie awake thinking of you, meditating on you through the night. Because you are my helper, I sing for joy in the shadow of your wings.

PSALM 63:6–7 NLT

Are you a worrier? Do you frequently find yourself working up a sweat building molehills into mountains during the midnight hours? This passage suggests an alternative for that nasty and unproductive habit. Instead of worrying, try meditating on the loving-kindness of God. Like a distressed chick tucked safely beneath the snug wings of the mother hen, allow the joy of being loved and protected to relax your tense muscles and ease you into peaceful rest.

Revitalization

Showers of Blessing

Do the skies themselves send
down showers? No, it is you,
O Lord our God. Therefore
our hope is in you, for you are
the one who does all this.

JEREMIAH 14:22 NIV

Have you ever stood in your parched
garden, praying for rain? The plants you've
nurtured from seeds are wilting, flower
petals litter the ground, fruit withers on the
vine. Then thunder clouds roll and the skies
burst forth with reinvigorating rain.

There will be dry times, too, in our
spiritual gardens, but our hope is
in the Lord our God, who sends
showers to revive us. Deluge
us today, Lord.

Snippets of Hope

*I also pray that you will understand
the incredible greatness of God's
power for us who believe him.*

EPHESIANS 1:19 NLT

Daydreams are snippets of hope for our
souls. Yearnings for something better,
something more exciting, something that
lifts our spirits. Some dreams are mere fancy,
but others are meant to last a lifetime because
God embedded them in our hearts. It's when
we lose sight of those dreams that hope dies.

But God offers us access to His almighty
power—the very same greatness that brought
His Son back from the dead. What
greater hope is there?

True Success

"For I know the plans I have for you,"
declares the LORD, "plans to prosper you
. . .plans to give you hope and a future."

JEREMIAH 29:11 NIV

As little girls, we dream about the handsome man we'll one day marry, exciting trips we'll take, the mansion we'll call home, and the beautiful, perfect children we'll have. A successful life—isn't that what we hope for?

But God doesn't call us to be successful; He calls us to trust Him. We may never be successful in the world's eyes, but trust in our Father's omnipotence ensures our future and our hope. And that's true success.

I Can't Lose!

Alive, I'm Christ's messenger;
dead, I'm his bounty. Life versus even
more life! I can't lose.

PHILIPPIANS 1:21 MSG

The old-timer smiled at his granddaughter as she rebuked him for driving the farm tractor. "Don't you know the danger at your age, Grandpa? You could be killed!"

"I'm not worried, darlin', and you shouldn't be either. What's the worst that could happen? I wake up in heaven. This life versus an even better one. . .for all eternity."

When worry begins to overshadow hope, remember three little words from Philippians: I can't lose!

Accolades

"Your Father, who sees what is done in secret, will reward you."

MATTHEW 6:4 NIV

The countless things we women do for our families are often not noticed or appreciated. What a comfort to know that our Father sees everything, no matter how small. Our reward may not be the Woman of the Year award, or even hugs and kisses. It may not be here on earth at all. I'm hoping it'll be a maid and cook for all eternity. But whatever it is, we'll be thrilled because our Father is pleased with us.

Salvation

Easy as ABC

God has done all this, so that we
will look for him and reach out and
find him. He isn't far from any of us.
ACTS 17:27 CEV

God is near. But we must reach out for
Him. There's a line that we choose to cross,
a specific action we take. We can't ooze into
the kingdom of God; it's an intentional
decision. It's simple, really—as simple as
ABC. *A* is Admitting we're sinful and in
need of a Savior. *B* is Believing that Jesus
died for our sins and rose from the grave.
C is Committing our lives to Him. Life
everlasting is then ours.

Best Seller

The mystery is that Christ
lives in you, and he is your hope
of sharing in God's glory.

COLOSSIANS 1:27 CEV

Everybody loves a good mystery—as long
as the plot twists a bit and the good guy wins
in the end. The Christian life is a mystery.
It's baffling that God could love us so deeply
that He sent His only Son to suffer and
die for us. And now the risen Christ lives
in our hearts, bridging the gap between us
and God forever. What an incredible
page-turner!

Beautify

For the LORD takes pleasure
in His people; He will beautify
the afflicted ones with salvation.

PSALM 149:4 NASB

My friend Anna is beautiful. The fact that she's suffered a stroke is insignificant. Her sweet spirit of faithfulness, generosity, and kindness, all couched in gentle humor, causes me to take pleasure in her company.

In the same way, our Lord takes pleasure in our company, despite our inabilities, unsightliness, or neediness. Hard to believe He actually chooses our company, but He does! And in spending time with us, He beautifies us with His lovely countenance.

Security

Survivor

*The terrible storm raged
for many days. . .until
at last all hope was gone.*

Following a lovely renewal of our wedding
vows on our tenth anniversary, my husband
and I boarded a Caribbean cruise ship.
Tragically, Hurricane Gilbert obliterated our
destination, Cancun, before hurling our ship
back and forth on twelve-foot waves for four
interminable days. I felt hopeless, sick as a
pup, and at the mercy of the storm.

Life's like that, isn't it? Unexpected
storms blow up, blot out the light,
and toss us about. But we are
survivors!

Living Hope

Now faith is being sure of what
we hope for and certain
of what we do not see.

HEBREWS 11:1 NIV

This beloved scripture has long been the Christian's definition of faith. But if reworked a smidge, it's also the meaning of hope in Christ: Hope is being sure of in whom we have placed our faith and certain of what we do not see. We don't see fragrance or love or blood flowing through our bodies, but we're certain of their existence. We can't see hope, but there's no doubt when it's alive within us. Praise God for living hope!

Band-Aids

We have run to God for safety.
Now his promises should greatly
encourage us to take hold of the
hope that is right in front of us.

HEBREWS 6:18 CEV

Have you ever lost your glasses or your keys and looked everywhere for them, only to have someone point out that they're right in front of you? God's hope is like that— right in front of us, but we don't always see it. Our eyes are too busy searching for things we think will infuse hope: financial security, makeovers, losing weight, marriage, a new baby. But these are only Band-Aids. Our true hope is in Christ alone.

Self-Control

Prune Juice, Anyone?

Therefore, prepare your minds for action; be self-controlled; set your hope fully on the grace to be given you when Jesus Christ is revealed.

1 PETER 1:13 NIV

Diets are the devil. They exclude chocolate éclairs and hinge on effective use of that dreaded *s* word: self-control. In the fruit bowl of the Spirit, self-control is the prune. It's hard to swallow but nonetheless essential to our faith—especially where hope is concerned. If self-control isn't exercised, we can find our spirits soaring up and down faster than the numbers on our bathroom scales. Like prunes, daily use of self-control regulates us and prepares us for action.

No Shame

No one whose hope is in you
will ever be put to shame.

PSALM 25:3 NIV

Some of us have A- temperaments.
We're not quite as flamboyant as type A
personalities or as pensive as type B, but
because of our tendency to rev our tongues
into overdrive before getting our brains in
gear, we spend a lot of time extracting foot
from mouth. God implores us to control our
tongues; the tiny sparks that inflame forests;
the rudders that control enormous
ships—our means of shame or
glorifying His name!

True Colors

May integrity and honesty
protect me, for I put my hope in you.
PSALM 25:21 NLT

At first the raven appeared solid black, but when she perched in a shaft of sunlight, her feathers shimmered in iridescent emerald, turquoise, and teal: her true colors.

We sometimes hide little acts of dishonesty—taking the bank's pen, pocketing that extra dollar from the clerk's mistake, fudging tax figures. But our integrity is on display at all times to the One who gave His life for us. When our true colors are exposed in the Son-light, we want to shimmer, too.

Creating a Chalice

"We live by faith, not by sight."
2 CORINTHIANS 5:7 NIV

Okay, so you popped a tire and the boss exploded because you were late for work again. Your dog upchucked in front of the dinner guests. Your daughter failed the big test. Your elderly mother fell and broke her hip. Bill collectors recite your number by heart. That's the outside. On the inside, God is sanding your sharp edges—impatience, frustration, worry—into a smooth chalice filled with His grace.

Aim High

My aim is to raise hopes by pointing
the way to life without end.

TITUS 1:2 MSG

No woman is an island. We're more like
peninsulas. Although we sometimes feel
isolated, we're connected to one another by
the roots of womanhood. We're all in this
together, girls. As we look around, we can't
help but see sisters who need a hand, a warm
smile, a caring touch. And especially hope.
People need hope, and if we know the Lord—
the source of eternal hope—it's up to us to
point the way through love.

Jump In

"You don't need more faith.
There is no 'more' or 'less' in faith.
If you have a bare kernel of faith,
say the size of a poppy seed, you
could say to this sycamore tree, 'Go
jump in the lake,' and it would do it."

LUKE 17:6 MSG

Luke 17:6 is an intriguing verse. Jesus
says there are no increments of faith. You
either have it or you don't. Having the faith
of Billy Graham or Mother Teresa may seem
unfathomable to us, but if we earnestly and
completely trust Jesus as our Savior, the
Bible says we already do. And God
is ready to work through our
lives as He has theirs.

Spiritual Growth

Integrity

"Is not your fear of God your confidence, and the integrity of your ways your hope?"

JOB 4:6 NASB

"Live your faith." These three little words are the goal of every Christian. Not "Don't smoke, cuss, or chew or hang around with those who do," or even "Be good so you'll get into heaven." Integrity begets behavior, not the other way around. We want to please our Lord by righteous behavior so we can fulfill the challenge of St. Francis of Assisi: "Preach the gospel at all times. Use words if necessary."

Glorious Awakening

I pray also that the eyes of your heart
may be enlightened in order that
you may know the hope to which
he has called you.

EPHESIANS 1:18 NIV

"Open the eyes of my heart, Lord. I want to see you." The lyrics of this beautiful praise song express our deepest desire—to truly see the hope before us. Like stereograms with 3-D images embedded within 2-D pictures (You know, those hidden images you can't see without squinting?), the glory and riches of following Christ are veiled to some because the eyes of their hearts are closed. Let us pray for our own spiritual awakening today.

Meet Me There

Christ gives me the strength
to face anything.
PHILIPPIANS 4:13 CEV

Most women dread going out alone—to
restaurants, shopping, social events—even
church. Sometimes we are the loneliest
when we're in a crowd. It's intimidating
to face a roomful of strangers. But it's well
worth it to bite the bullet and just go to
that church brunch or spiritual retreat or
Bible Study. I would have missed some
awesome blessings if I hadn't gone (alone)
to many spiritual events. I found I did know
somebody after all. Jesus met me there.

Strength

Fly Me Away

But those who hope in the
LORD will renew their strength.
They will soar on wings like eagles;
they will run and not grow weary,
they will walk and not be faint.

ISAIAH 40:31 NIV

On those weary days when our chins drag
the ground, when our feet are stuck fast
in the quagmire of everyday responsibility,
this verse becomes our hope and our prayer:
Mount me up with wings like eagles, Father,
fly me away! Let my spirit soar above the
clouds on the winds of your strength.
Make me strong as a marathon
runner, continuing mile
after mile after mile. Be my
tailwind, Lord. Amen.

Fill 'Er Up

"What strength do I have,
that I should still hope?"

JOB 6:11 NIV

Run, rush, hurry, dash: a typical American woman's day. It's easy to identify with David's lament in Psalm 22:14 NASB: "I am poured out like water. . .my heart is like wax; it is melted within me." Translation: I'm pooped; I'm numb; I'm drained dry. When we are at the end of our strength, God doesn't want us to lose hope of the refilling He can provide if we only lift our empty cups to Him.

Reboot

Be strong in the Lord
and in his mighty power.

EPHESIANS 6:10 NLT

The toilet overflows, check bounces, temper flies, scale shows a three pound gain, kids stampede, husband forgets again. . . .

Ever have one of those days? How marvelous that when we're at our weakest point, our Lord is at His strongest, and He gladly shares that strength with us. He won't necessarily fix the plumbing, but He will reboot our attitudes.

Thankfulness

Fearfully Made

You knit me together in my mother's womb. I praise you because I am fearfully and wonderfully made.

PSALM 139:13–14 NIV

Crow's feet, frizzy hair, saddle bags, big feet—most women dislike something about their bodies. We feel much more fearfully than wonderfully made. But God loves us just as we are. He wants us to look past the wrinkles and see laugh footprints; to use those knobby knees for praying and age-spotted hands for serving. And in the process, praise Him for limbs that move, eyes that see, and ears that hear His Word.

All in the Family

We are God's house,
if we keep our courage
and remain confident in
our hope in Christ.

HEBREWS 3:6 NLT

Just as our children gain their identity from being an integral part of our household, we proudly bear the identity of our Father's house. What an honor! To be a member of God's household! To even take out the garbage or clean our rooms is a privilege.

Send Me a Sign

Let your unfailing love surround us,
LORD, for our hope is in you alone.

PSALM 33:22 NLT

With deadlines and schedules swirling in my head while driving down the interstate, I did a double take at the car passing me. A white-painted message across the back passenger window grabbed my attention: I AM LOVED. Wow. So am I. It only took a moment to thank Papa God for His unfailing love, but a smile lit my face all day. A simple but profound reminder is all we need from time to time.

No Greater Comfort

"O death, where is your victory?
O death, where is your sting?"

1 CORINTHIANS 15:55 NLT

There's no denying that the loss of a loved one stings. Our hearts burn, sear, and ache with pain. But Christ's victory over death after His crucifixion enables His followers to experience that same victory. We, too, will stand as conquerors of the grave, arm in arm with believers who have gone before us. What greater hope? What greater comfort?

Laugh a Rainbow

"When I see the rainbow in
the clouds, I will remember
the eternal covenant between God
and every living creature on earth."

GENESIS 9:16 NLT

Ever feel like a cloud is hanging over your
head? Sometimes the cloud darkens to the
color of bruises, and we're deluged with cold
rain that seems to have no end. When you're
in the midst of one of life's thunderstorms,
tape this saying to your mirror: Cry a river,
laugh a rainbow. The rainbow, the symbol
of hope that God gave Noah after the flood,
reminds us even today that every storm will
eventually pass.

Asking Why?

But the needy will not always
be forgotten, nor the hope
of the afflicted ever perish.

PSALM 9:18 NIV

Why me? Why is God allowing this to happen? Why doesn't He intervene? When we're in the midst of a difficult time, it's easy to forget that God is not the afflicter, but is the helper and healer of the afflicted. He is not cracking the whip, but feels every stripe inflicted on our backs by a sin-filled world—just like those of His only Son, Jesus.

Trust

Tune In

And hope does not disappoint us,
because God has poured out his love
into our hearts by the Holy Spirit,
whom he has given to us.

ROMANS 5:5 NIV

Is your spiritual antenna tuned in to the Holy
Spirit? The Holy Spirit is the communicator
of the trinity: our helper, comforter, and
instructor. Through Him, God pours love and
hope into us. Like radio waves broadcasting
invisibly through the atmosphere, the Holy
Spirit communicates to believers. We must,
however, make the effort to tune in our
receivers to His frequency, and then choose
to obey His guidance—even when it's
inconvenient.

Test-a-moany of Praise

Why are you in despair, O my soul?
And why have you become
disturbed within me? Hope in God,
for I shall yet praise him.

PSALM 42:11 NASB

It's said that a testimony is the result
of a test with a lot of moaning. We all
endure hardship in this life, and most of
us are quick to vocalize our despair. God
understands. His own Son cried out "My
God, my God, why hast thou forsaken me?"
in His darkest moment on the cross. But
hope knows there is a victorious day ahead
when we will yet praise Him. It's Friday,
and Sunday is coming.

Saints Preserve Us

I will praise you in
the presence of your saints.
PSALM 52:9 NIV

We sing, "Lord, I want to be in that
number, when the saints go marching in!"
But who exactly are saints? Exceptionally
good people like Saint Nicholas or Mother
Teresa? The Bible calls all true believers
saints. Some think if their derriere simply
graces a pew, they're in. But sitting in
church no more makes you a Christian than
standing in your closet makes you a vacuum
cleaner. Only dedicated Christ-lovers will
march into heaven. Are you in that number?

Grab and Run

Abraham called the name
of that place The Lord Will Provide.

GENESIS 22:14 NASB

Abraham was asked to do the unthinkable:
sacrifice his only son. Can you imagine
the terrible struggle he went through in
deciding whether to obey God or grab his
boy and run? But he chose to exercise his
faith and trust that God would provide a
way out. And He did. What's really in our
hearts is revealed during crises. Do we trust
God enough to put the lives of our
beloved in His hands?

Truth

If You Build it, He Will Come

Do not snatch your word
of truth from me, for your
regulations are my only hope.

PSALM 119:43 NLT

Bibles wear and tear. Papers get discarded.
Hard drives crash. But memorizing
scripture assures us that God's Word will
never be lost. His truth will always be at our
disposal, any moment of the day or night
when we need a word of encouragement, of
guidance, of hope. Like a phone call from
heaven, our Father communicates to us via
scripture implanted in our hearts.

But it is up to us to build the signal
tower.

Prince on a White Steed

*I promise that from that day on,
you will call me your husband
instead of your master.*

HOSEA 2:16 CEV

I have two husbands. If you're a Christ-lover and married, you do, too. The Bible considers believers "the bride of Christ" and draws many parallels to a marital relationship (Ephesians 5:25). Christ provides for and protects His people. And even better than many flawed human marriages, He loves us unconditionally and refuses to divorce us no matter what. He's our prince on a white steed. . .forever.

Looming Large

And Isaiah's word: There's the root
of our ancestor Jesse, breaking
through the earth and growing
tree tall, tall enough for everyone
everywhere to see and take hope!

ROMANS 15:12 MSG

I'll never forget my first view of a giant sequoia on a vacation to the Northwest. Dwarfed by the towering tree, I felt the magnitude of the Ancient of Days. The enormous tree was visible for miles, like a skyscraper against the flat horizon.

Isaiah likened Jesus to a tree like that— tall enough for everyone everywhere to see and take hope. And yet some miss Him. She who has eyes to see, let her see!

Wholeness

Blameless

[Jesus] has brought you into
his own presence, and you are
holy and blameless as you stand
before him without a single fault.

COLOSSIANS 1:22 NLT

Holiness. Wouldn't we all like to attain
it? But it's impossible. Even if we shave our
heads, eat only birdseed, forsake makeup
and wear nothing but mumus, we still
wouldn't be holy. We'd just be ugly. The
only way we can achieve holiness is through
Jesus, who by His death on our behalf
ushers us into the presence of God,
blameless, beautiful, and whole.
And we can leave our mumus
at home.

Whole and Healed

Pray for each other so that you
can live together whole and healed.
The prayer of a person living right
with God is something powerful
to be reckoned with.

JAMES 5:16 MSG

Do you have soul siblings? Brothers and
sisters in Christ? Caring people who pray
for you and with you about, well, everything?
Like a life preserver in a turbulent sea,
prayer partners are buoyancy for the soul
and security through any storm. Heart-
bonds, once established, create a trusting
environment where we can bare our souls
before the Lord in mutual prayer to become
whole and healed. Prayer partners
are warm hugs from God.

Mosaic Masterpieces

God gives us what it takes
to do all that we do.

2 CORINTHIANS 3:5 CEV

As an orthopedic occupational therapist, I work with broken people. Lives are forever altered by strokes, accidents, disease. "I can't live like this" is a phrase often uttered at the beginning of the rehabilitation journey. But we don't know just how many ways we can live until we depend on God to give us what we need. Not only to live, but live productive, fulfilling lives. He creates mosaic masterpieces from the broken pieces of our lives.

Wisdom

Slathered in SPF

You are my refuge and my shield;
I have put my hope in your word.
PSALM 119:114 NIV

These days, the word *shield* evokes images of glistening sunbathers dotting beaches and carefree children slathered in sunscreen. Like the psalmist's metal shield, sunscreen deflects dangerous rays, preventing them from penetrating vulnerable skin—higher SPF for more protection. When we are immersed in God's Word, we erect a shield that deflects Satan's attempts to penetrate our weak flesh. Internalizing more of God's Word creates a higher SPF: Scripture Protection Factor. Are you well-coated?

Double Scoop

Know also that wisdom is
sweet to your soul; if you find it,
there is a future hope for you.

PROVERBS 24:14 NIV

Chocolate chunk cookies. Sock-it-to-me
pound cake. Ice cream sundaes with cherries
on top. Sweets add zest to the mundane,
don't they? (Not to mention cellulite to the
thighs!) In the same way, wisdom enhances
our souls. What kind of wisdom? Not
mathematical equations, science facts, or
Latin verbs. No, the wisdom embedded in
God's Word is what sweetens our
spirits and adds zing to our
mundane lives. How about a
double scoop today?

Choosing Last

Do you see a man
wise in his own eyes?
There is more hope for
a fool than for him.

PROVERBS 26:12 NASB

When my first national article was published, I proudly stood in the middle of a bookstore, held the magazine aloft, and announced that this was my article and my picture. One kind elderly lady smiled but everyone else simply ignored me. It was a painful lesson in humility. Humility is a learned skill, not an inborn trait. That's why Jesus taught about choosing the mindset of humility. The last shall be first.

The Foundation and Finale

I hope to see you soon,
and then we will talk face to face.
Peace be with you.

3 John 1:14–15 NLT

My prayer is that the message you receive from this book is that Christ is the ultimate source of hope. We can live without many things, but we cannot live without hope. It's the air we breathe, the water that invigorates every molecule of our being, the motivation that drives us. Hope enriches and empowers us, connecting us with our Papa God. Hope is the essence of our faith. It's the foundation and the finale.

Scripture Index

Psalms

Proverbs

John

Acts

Romans

Notes